I HARDLY
KNEW ME

I HARDLY KNEW ME

FOLLOWING LOVE, FAITH, AND SKITTLES TO A TRANSGENDER AWAKENING

NIA CHIARAMONTE

lakedrivebooks.com

Lake Drive Books
6757 Cascade Road SE, #162
Grand Rapids, MI 49546

info@lakedrivebooks.com
lakedrivebooks.com
@lakedrivebooks

Publishing books that help you heal, grow, and discover.

Paperback ISBN: 978-1-957687-59-9
E-book ISBN: 978-1-957687-60-5

Library of Congress Control Number: 2025906543

Cover design by Laura Duffy

Contents

Introduction

This is the first time I've done this. No, not write a book. I "accidentally" wrote my first book, a children's book, *The Story of Nib*, a few years back. I'm talking about what I'm doing right now. This is the first time I've written in the middle of the night. I'm tired. I should be asleep. I have five kids, seven right now because my nieces are staying over, who will most likely choose this morning to get up at 3:30 a.m. and be awake for the day. The first one just woke up due to my typing. Fortunately, it was the oldest, who I convinced to go back to bed, but I still can't sleep. I need to get this out of me.

It's 3:30 a.m., and like many of the other moments in this book, this one is just here, begging to get out. Quite frankly, I'm not sure why it couldn't wait until morning, but it kept pounding away at my brain until, after an hour, I decided to get out of bed and let it out.

It's perfect really, because that's what this book is: a collection of moments. Just as I didn't set out to write my first book, I didn't set out to write this book either. What started as a single moment in time, weeping in my living room, needing to process my emotions, has come together to highlight an eight-year span of my life. This eight-year "moment" in my life has been a big one. I've undergone a transformation.

For those who have stuck with me, they'll recognize the person who they used to know as someone who has grown so much that I'm almost unrecognizable. Except that I'm the same. That's the thing about transition and growth. We take pieces of ourselves with us, both good and bad. Even if we try to burn away the bad things, the hard things, they leave scars on us. Many moments along the way make us who we are right now, in this present moment. And right now, in this present moment, I'm writing. You're reading.

If you found yourself here, maybe because someone gave you this book, or maybe because you're going through your own transformation, or maybe because we know each other, it doesn't matter. You're here now. And really, that's all we have. This present moment.

If you've read other memoirs about transgender people (spoiler alert: I'm transgender), or other memoirs period, you'll recognize most memoirs as a collection of moments in time. I hope though that this one is unique, in that it documents my transformation in real time. I have changed from someone who was so inside myself that I could barely look people in the eye, and definitely couldn't order pizza over the phone for the first twenty-five years of my life for fear of sounding stupid, to someone who is moving toward being fully alive in this present moment, unfettered by what others think, writing about my life for all to judge. Even at 4:00 a.m.

For me, the past eight years of my transformation have been made up of present moments. They've been both exceedingly freeing and excruciatingly painful at almost the same time. Many of the moments I've captured here are happening in real time for me, just like this one. Okay, all moments happen in real time, I get it, but these stories were written as I experienced the emotion of the moment. My hope is that you feel them. All the joy, pain, loss, dysphoria, freedom, abandonment, hope, love, grief, and euphoria. I hope you can feel each moment as I did. And no, I don't want you to get super depressed by reading this book, but I do hope you can experience what it's like for a transgender person to come into their own in the world. I hope you can feel the finding of self and the waking up to new life that we all desire.

When I first came out to my family, one of my closest family members said to me, "The only thing people will think about you in the future is that you're transgender." And while I told him he was wrong and that I am more than this one piece of me, part of what he said was right. People judge. And people judge the first thing they can judge about you. For me, it's typically that I'm transgender. They usually don't get to know me well enough to judge me on other parts of my life, or maybe just well enough to drop their judgment of me altogether. For those that do drop their judgment, they may get to see all of me.

I used to be so hidden that even I couldn't see who I was. I was so repressed in my body and I merged my external personality with anyone I met, because it was easier than exploring within and because I hated conflict (where are my Enneagram 9s?)[1].

Now, those that see me will see a confident person, (mostly) at home in their body. Someone who loves life, to the point of getting up at 4:25 a.m. to write about it.

And for those who continue reading this book, I hope you too will be able to drop the judgment you have. About me. About transgender people. About yourself. And be here now.

Many of the moments here are heavy and thick with emotion, and you might think some of the moments included here are too minor, too uninfluential on the overarching narrative of life to be included in a memoir. But for me, those are the moments that are apropos of everything. They are the moments that made me who I am, right now, at 4:30 a.m. (still no kids are awake, thank God).

These are the moments that shape all of us if we let them. They shaped me. They are the moments where we can get to know ourselves. Before I started this journey, I hardly knew me. I was unexplored. So much so that,

---

1   The Enneagram of Personality is a personality theory that classifies people into nine types based on how they relate to the world, based on motivation, not just behavior. For more information check out the Enneagram Institute online at www.enneagraminstitute.com. I also recommend Suzanne Stabile and Ian Morgan Cron's book, *The Road Back to You*, as a starter.

now, eight years later, many of the things I believed/thought/loved when I started writing have changed to the point that they are unrecognizable. There are some major themes that have gotten me through, and you'll recognize a lot of self-encouragement. Some of what you read here was written by someone who, looking back, felt like a different person. You may find these inconsistencies in belief or the way I have written down these stories from moment to moment jarring, but I urge you to see them as growth. Live transformation happening right in front of you.

I would be remiss if I didn't acknowledge the political context present during the publishing of this book. A time where trans people are under fire from a political faction influenced by conservative evangelical voters, creating legislation that is literally killing people. Much has been written about this, but I hope to give insight into what daily life is like for a trans person, so people can stop believing the myths and stories made up to perpetuate a narrative about us, and instead listen to what we are saying. Things will get better if we choose to listen.

Thank you for going on this journey with me. As we know, it's not about the destination, it's about the journey. But also, we're here now. A momentary destination. For me, 4:45 a.m. on a Monday morning, hoping I can get another hour of sleep before work. For you, wherever you are, hoping to relax with a good, illuminating (and hopefully at times funny) book.

Together in the fullness of our humanity we can make the world a better place. Reflecting ourselves back to one another. Because ultimately that's what love does. It shows us who we are. And while we may not know each other, in the end I want you to feel loved. I want you to know you deserve to be happy. I want you to feel what I have felt so that you can have more empathy for those around you and also more empathy for yourself. Because we are the hardest on ourselves. And until we can love ourselves for who we are, we can't fully be here now.

Thanks again for joining me on this journey. At this destination. Thanks for being in the both/and of life with me. I hope to meet you someday and hear all about what you were doing when you read about the day I was up at 4:50 a.m. Still no kids awake. Thank goodness.

Peace and Love,
Nia

Hope

I sit down to write this with my spouse weeping in the other room. I had to abandon her though, in her time of need, because I needed to get this out of my body. I needed to express my faith in God, my need to search for hope in the midst of the pain created by well-intentioned people and a religious machine.

It took me twenty minutes to write that.

My emotions are swirling at such a breakneck pace these days. I thought I was getting healthy when I learned to cry in therapy over a year ago. Now I don't know. It seems like things would have been a lot better if I had continued to live life unaffected. Unaffected by people and unaffected by religion. My faith was strong. But once I found a God who loved me, everything changed. I'm not talking about finding a God who loved me in spite of who I am, but a God who loved me because of who I am. The moment I realized that God loved me, I couldn't go back. I had to move forward. For me that meant confronting what had been there all along. I was transgender and I knew it, even though I hadn't let myself see it for fear of damnation.

I no longer have that fear of damnation in a life to come. No, I'm focused on the now, and the now is crushing me to death.

Religion . . .

People . . .

Shit.

Crushing the breath of life out of me.

I have to write this for the sake of hope. I have to start something that needs to be finished. If I can come back to this, continuing to move forward, it means hope is real. It means something has changed. Maybe something in me, maybe something in others, maybe both. But ultimately it means all of this wasn't for nothing. It means there is hope in the world.

The thing is, I know there is hope. At least I think there is. I'm actually an optimist. I had a marquee sign in my office for the longest time that had a quote from Anne Frank that read, "Despite everything, I believe that people are really good at heart."

People are good. I believe in my core that we are this way because that is how we were created. In the image of a God who loves. But damn, people are really trying to prove that statement wrong right now. I want to focus on all the good things in my life. The relationships that are flourishing, my five kids who are thriving, my marriage which has never been stronger . . . but I can't. I'm buried alive.

I am broken sitting on the couch, early in the morning, and my wife lies weeping in the other room. Not because of anything we've done to each other but because of forces outside of our marriage and ourselves. A world that doesn't want trans people to exist and a narrow religious system not made for everyone. I hope this story is one that continues to move forward. I want to be self-sacrificing and say I hope this is the case for other trans people who follow behind me, but I truly hope that is the case for me. I hope that is the case for my marriage and my kids.

Because life without hope is . . . hopeless.

There it is, that dry wit that has been buried finally shows signs of life.

I used to not be able to feel my body. Through years of shutting down my emotions I thought everything was fine. Sure, I'd get the occasional back spasm, but I was strong. I was resilient. Nothing got me down. That was then.

Fyodor Dostoevsky, nineteenth century Russian novelist once said: "To live without hope is to cease to live." I feel that getting closer. But sitting down to write this means there is a little hope left in me, even though I can't really see it. I feel it . . . somewhere.

Thirty-Four

I was a huge jerk. That is how it all started.

When someone gives you a birthday gift, you're supposed to say thank you and appear grateful. In fact, you should *be* grateful. Especially when that someone who gave you the gift, your spouse, is desperately trying to show you how much they care about and see you for who you are.

It was my birthday, and I got a gift from my spouse Katie, showing me how much she saw who I was and how much she loved me. And instead of seeing it for what it was, the beautiful show of unending love from someone who sees me and knows me, instead of thanking her for it, I complained.

I was a jerk.

Let me explain.

I am a creature of comfort, and Katie knows that. She knows I love sitting in the warm sun in a field of green, just soaking it in. If I could lie in a hammock for my job, I would. (Is that a thing? Surely someone has a job as a hammock tester.). Or sitting with a warm robe in front of a crackling fire. (Robe tester or fireplace tester surely has to be a job, right?) Currently I am sitting in the warm sun in a green field right now, wearing a silk robe and a fleece sweatshirt.

No, I'm not kidding.

I love to be comfortable. I think I've even passed this gene down to my kids. Once, unsolicited, my eight-year-old daughter told me she wanted to be Santa Claus. Not for the typical reasons mind you, like bringing people gifts, making people smile, riding reindeer, being able to shrink down and go through the chimney, or even the all-the-milk-and-cookies-you-can-eat perk. No, she wanted to be Santa Claus because, and I quote, "You get to stay up past eight and wear a robe all the time." So needless to say, this trait is inside me.

I've been this way as long as I can remember. I'm not sure how I acquired this drive to be physically comfortable. I think it has something to do with the grounding of it. The physical cocooning inside the comfort. I remember when I was four years old and the monsters were surely creating battle plans under my bed, I would pull the covers up and over my head into a tight shield with only the nose-hole exposed to those that would do me harm (hey, a kid's gotta breathe, and if they get my nose, I guess, oh well).

I crave serenity in all shapes and forms. Reading a good book, fishing, napping, sleeping, more napping, swinging on swings, floating in a pool, and wearing comfortable clothes. Oh the comfortable clothes I have. For me, there's just nothing like snuggling into a piece of clothing that is so comfortable it makes me feel safe.

And Katie, bless her heart, she knew this about me too. She knew I'd do anything for a soft pair of pants and a cozy blanket. So that's why she got me a great birthday gift that I should have been thankful for.

It was my thirty-fourth birthday, you know that special one where it doesn't matter at all? Katie, though, was thoroughly thoughtful and made us reservations at a Mexican restaurant for drinks and appetizers and then at an upscale restaurant for dinner. In fact, I just looked back at that day on our calendar and the date was listed as "Hope when you need it most." Little did she know how true that was.

The problem in all her planning, though, lay in the fact that margaritas were two dollars. I swear I only had two of them, two and a half max. But by the time we got in the car to head to dinner (don't worry, she was driving) and she gave me my gift, my inner child was sitting in the passenger seat of that car just wanting to be seen. You know the moment.

When you yell at someone for no good reason, only to find out through years of therapy that your little-self needed something. I know I am not in this club alone.

I opened the present, completely unsure of what it was, although she had been talking it up all night. To my surprise, it was undershirts and pajama pants. Not regular undershirts and pajama pants mind you, but the comfortable, soft kind. The kind most guys would say in a deep, gruff voice, "Uh, what are you trying to say about me?" I think the word *luxurious* was actually printed on the packaging of both items.

Katie proceeded to explain to me that she knew I liked comfort. She knew I liked soft clothing. She also knew I used to wear women's clothing occasionally when I was younger. (Did I forget to mention that?)

This was my secret I had exposed to her about a year into our marriage. I think we were lying in bed, weirdly at my parents' house, as we were visiting from college one weekend, and I told her. It was something about how I used to express myself through women's clothing, completely underplaying the significance of this gender expression in my life and making it clear that I certainly, mostly, probably, never would, kind of not, be interested in this type of gender expression going forward. And on my thirty-fourth birthday, Katie, knowing me more than I knew myself, wanted me to know that she saw me.

She saw all of me, even that part of me that I was hiding from the rest of the world. The part that she knew was deeply connected to my wholeness. She saw my feminine side, which came out more when I snuggled down with a good book in a nice robe.

Maybe it was the two (and a half) margaritas, but more likely it was the feeling of being exposed that tag-teamed in my little-self, the one who needed to be seen but couldn't accept it, who in turn tag-teamed in my jerk-self.

I immediately launched into a diatribe about how, while it was a thoughtful gift, it wasn't enough. I wanted more. More softness, more femininity. I'm not sure how this came off to her because I was basically telling her I wished she had really seen what was going on with me. Even though I myself couldn't completely see what was going on with me, I had hoped that she could. She succeeded though, better than I was willing to admit, and now I was exposed, uncertain of who I was underneath my thirty-four-year-old facade. Since she exposed me, couldn't she also tell me what was going on with me? Was that too much to ask?!

I'm asked all the time, *"Did you know your whole life, or did you just figure this out?"* This is the single most common question I get about my gender transition.

This has in fact been with me my whole life, but to say I knew what was going on would be disingenuous. Initially when I came out to friends, there were multiple people who said to me, *"I think that makes sense based on some of my interactions with you."* And while they can never quite say which interactions showed them I was a woman living life as a man, this is almost exactly how I feel about my own life—that it makes sense based on what I know about myself.

Looking back, there were points in my life that I see in hindsight as signposts for what was to come, but in the moment, there was no way for me to put any of that together.

I grew up in an uber religious evangelical Christian culture. Church on Sunday morning, Sunday night, Wednesday night, and thinking about church the other five days of the week while attending an evangelical Christian school. All while trying not to get *left behind* during the Rapture. No explanation needed for the former fundamentalists among us, but in case you don't know, that's where, at some unknown point in the future, Jesus comes back on the clouds and whisks away the true believers, leaving only (for some reason) neat piles of clothing around. Why he needs to take them naked I'll never know, but it made all us kids scared every time we got home from school and laundry was folded on the couch and no one else was around. Like really genuinely scared.

Needless to say, most if not all my feelings about my own gender differences that surfaced during my childhood were flung immediately into the abyss, without much inspection. It's like when society used to view left-handedness as a sin. We'd tell kids they were right-handed even when they weren't. I felt like the kid who thought they were right-handed because everyone told them they were right-handed. I learned to act and behave like a man, quite well in fact, but something felt off. For me, something didn't quite feel complete.

So, thirty-four years of repression and living up to other people's expectations came spilling out in one fell swoop on my wife. I knew (or thought I knew) our love could handle it. I instinctively knew she would give me the space to understand what I didn't even know I was telling her. Also, she was the one person in my life who I knew was safe. And the safety that she provided to me that night, ironically, led me to be a real jerk. Little did we both know that the safety she provided to me, my hurt little-self, and my protesting jerk-self, would lead me down a path. The force of my response let her in on who I was that night, even though I still didn't know what that meant.

Letting a loved one in is different than coming out. When I came out to Katie, I told her who I was. This is me, a transgender woman. But on my thirty-fourth birthday, when I first let Katie in, even with an emotional outburst, I was asking her to help me. I needed someone to provide a space where I could be safe to get to know myself better. We all need someone like this in our lives. Someone who reflects us back to ourselves, so even when we don't know ourselves, we can explore who we are in a loving, safe space. A space where we can be free. I'm so grateful for the way she saw me that night, even if I initially rejected it. I'm grateful for the way she has seen me our entire lives, because that seeing has led me to my freedom.

Love

She was an image of beauty frozen in my mind. She wore a pink two-piece chiffon dress, bedazzled with pink sequins extending throughout her thick, shoulder-length hair. I was so nervous as we hopped into the limo and headed to the dance. My stomach churned as the limo pulled out of the long driveway. I thought I might puke all over the clean black leather and ruin the night before it even began. But I made it through, including the dancing (not Christian-school-sponsored dancing of course, but unfunded-by-the-school-after-party, PG-rated dancing), the after-party where we bowled our hearts out in our fancy outfits, and the 2:00 a.m. breakfast at the early morning after-after-party eatery of choice for high school kids in our home city of Des Moines, Iowa.

But when we pulled up to her front door, tired from a fantastic ten hours of partying, my stomach turned again. What was I going to do? How was this going to go?

I'm pretty sure if the God of our fundamental religious community hadn't been involved, it would have been a more fun end to a fun night (thanks a lot Joshua Harris and *I Kissed Dating Goodbye*[2]). It didn't matter though; we were in love. I promptly asked her to be my girlfriend, and she said yes. We sealed the deal with . . . a high five. A holy high five to be exact. And that was the end of our junior prom and the first real date between me and my wife Katie.

---

2 In 2024, Joshua Harris suggested you not read his book, *I Kissed Dating Goodbye* (Multnomah Books, 1997).

But it was really three years before that when we went to a concert together that I fell in love. I should clarify, we didn't go to the concert *together*. Yes, we spent an hour and a half together, sitting on the floor of an old church van with five or six other kids, but it wasn't a date. In fact, Katie doesn't even remember I was there.

But no matter, I fell in love that night.

There was one specific moment I looked at her, eighth-grade fist held high in the air, keeping time to the beat of Geoff Moore and the Distance (if you know, you know), and I knew. I saw her fully in that moment, and I fell in love. I felt that I knew who she was entirely, and I wanted to be with her forever. No, I'm not exaggerating.

This wasn't your typical love story though. You know, the one where lovers' eyes meet from across the room at a concert during a sweet rendition of "Breakfast" by the Newsboys (yes, this was a kick-ass concert) and all else fades away but two beating hearts in love. No, ours is a story of friendship. We were already friends before that concert. And over the next few years, we became best friends.

We'd talk on the phone for hours, me sprinkling in sound effects on my voice-FX Nickelodeon phone. We would talk about crushes, and even though we both liked each other off and on, we never said that. She was someone, the only one in fact, who listened to me. She really heard me when we talked. At the time, I didn't know who I was (do any of us in eighth grade?). All I knew was that I was different, and I also knew she could see me. She even got close to uncovering all of me a few times throughout the years.

Once, a few years after we started dating, we were lying on my couch watching a *20/20* special about gender nonconformity and "men" who shopped in the women's section. You can imagine how this segment in the late 1990s portrayed these married couples. It wasn't great, but progressive for its time. At one moment during the special, Katie, with her head on my chest, turned to me and said, *"You're not interested in something like that are you?"* Not an accusatory question but a curious question. I remember my heart starting to pound through my chest, threatening to throw her off me and across the room. I wanted to turn to her and scream, *YES!* But I didn't know why, so I said in my deepest, manliest voice, "Oh no, of course not."

I still didn't know.

Fast forward fifteen years to my thirty-fourth birthday and she got so much closer. And even though my outburst on my thirty-fourth birthday helped, I still didn't know who I was. It was only a few months later, though, that things truly changed.

I had become aware that something about me was different. Katie and 20/20 had done a great job of mirroring pieces of myself back to me so I could see who I was, but I still wasn't fully sure what was going on, so I suggested a weekend away for us. No kids. Romantic hotel. Relaxing weekend. No stress, just us. I, however, had a slightly ulterior motive.

We traveled from our home in Iowa about six hours north to Delafield, Wisconsin, to stay at the swanky Delafield Hotel. I chose this small Wisconsin town not only due to the amazing accommodations but due to its proximity to Milwaukee, which happened to be where the nearest Hamburger Mary's franchise chain was. If you don't know, Hamburger Mary's is the nation's foremost (and only?) fast-food burger, drag restaurant. Their slogan is "Eat, Drink, and be . . . Mary."

I wanted to try being Mary, in public. I needed to know for sure what was going on inside me. So, I booked us the hotel, dinner, and activities, including a trip to Hamburger Mary's. Now my memory is a bit fuzzy, but I think I asked if Katie would be okay if we went to Hamburger Mary's, though she may have a different recollection and may say that I just scheduled it without getting her input. Okay, I may have done that.

Either way, we were booked, and I was freaked. I bought a dress and wig online. I bought shoes at Goodwill (the favorite store of trans people everywhere) and brought some makeup from home. I was ready. I was going to do this. I needed to do this.

Truly going out in public expressing my inner self outwardly was terrifying, but it also felt mostly right. I say mostly because there was and is a certain aspect to drag and putting on a persona that didn't quite meet the need of my transgender self looking to find herself. There's a performance aspect to it. And while it was super fun, papering over my male facade with another facade didn't feel quite right somehow. I look back on this memory now, though, as a pivotal moment. It was a moment I was able to find my Knowing, as Glennon Doyle calls it in her wonderful book *Untamed*, because my wife gave me the space to do so.

To hear Katie tell this story, she was terrified. In one swift moment, she went from having a husband holding her hand to having a wife on her arm. You can imagine all the emotions that may come with something like that. Not to mention the fact that I accidentally parked down a dark alley and we had to walk three blocks to the restaurant at 9:00 p.m., me wobbling in heels the whole way. Oops.

It ended up being a pivotal moment for my gender journey. Not only was it the first time I had gone out in public like this, but it was the first time I had been at a drag show. As we sat and ate delicious hamburgers, watching the performers sing and dance around the restaurant for the bachelorette and birthday parties, I had a realization. Although I felt like I was sitting there in drag along with the performers, that was not who I was. I didn't know who I was, but I was starting to know who I wasn't. I wasn't a drag performer, and I wasn't a man.

It took me another two years to come out to myself as transgender. During that time, I experimented with gender expression—a lot—while Katie gave me space. Just like I had seen her at that concert so many years before, she saw something true about me even then. She may not have known exactly what, but she gave me space to be and explore it. When I finally did come out to myself, I was able to see all the times (there were so many) that my relationship with Katie allowed me to be who I am. That's what pure, perfect love does. It gives us back to ourselves. It allows us to feel safe inside ourselves. Only when we feel safe can we start to understand who we really are at the core.

While Katie showed me what love was, I still had to start loving myself to fully find out who I was. To do this, I had to surround myself with amazing people who saw me and gave me the grace and safety to move forward. That space was necessary to combat the shame, fear, worthlessness, and doubt. When we surround ourselves with safe people, no matter what part of ourselves we're searching for, we're able to give more of that safety to ourselves as well. I had that space, and each day, my Knowing was getting a little stronger.

Transition in the Dark

As I drove home from therapy on the stretch of interstate where I-80 and I-35 join to become the same road for a moment before branching off again toward the rest of the country, my mind raced. What would I do? What would I say? I had realized that morning that I was transgender. How should I tell my wife Katie, who I loved so much? I didn't want to hurt her or have her think I had withheld this information purposely our whole lives.

I had started my journey with therapy months earlier and at the time didn't have any clue where to begin. I ended up googling *gender, therapist, Des Moines, IA*. Turned out I lived in a big enough, progressive enough small city to have a good choice of therapists who specialize in gender issues. I chose one, mostly at random (aside from making sure they also understood spirituality issues), and made an appointment, thinking full well I'd cancel before I went.

But when the time came for me to go, I didn't cancel. Katie and I had already had too many conversations about the topic for me to think I didn't need professional help. I reluctantly went and told the therapist I was there because, well, I didn't know. I liked to express myself by wearing women's clothes? I liked to express myself by wearing women's clothes, and my wife now knew about it? Or was it, I liked to express myself by wearing women's clothes, and my wife knew about it, and I was also pretty sure this was about much more than clothing? Yeah, that was the one.

My first therapist, a kind, short woman with gentle eyes, didn't take too long to get to the bottom of the excuse heap, discarding such beauties as, *I wear these things to feel good, it helps me relieve stress,* and the ever popular, *I just do it because I like it.* And when she did, it was so matter-of-fact, not some big pronouncement. She asked a question, I answered it, and she responded with something like, "And what does that mean for you?"

"I'm transgender," I said almost without thinking.

It was obvious to me. It had been obvious to me the whole time; I had just refused to look it in the eye. Once I did, I suddenly knew so much more, and the fears started to spread. What did this mean? No really, now what was going to happen to my marriage? I knew it could survive the occasional gender-bending when it came to clothing, but I didn't know what being transgender would mean for our relationship. After discovering a huge part of my identity that morning in therapy, I was excited, but not enough to quell the fears as they started to spread like wildfire, consuming everything that dared get in their way. I was hoping for the best, planning for the worst, only seeing far enough down the road to take the next step. I was in the liminal space. I wondered how to take the next step when it seemed like there was no ground beneath me. As I drove on the interstate, wondering what I would say to her, I thought back to another episode of 20/20.

An exposé in the mid-90s: *How to take your penis, turn it inside out, and make it a vagina and become the woman you've always wanted to be.*

Yeah, I'm sure that's what it was titled.

The program depicted the burgeoning medical practice of "sex change operations" at a time when gender confirmation surgery (GCS) and gender affirmation surgery (GAS) had not yet made their way into the popular lexicon. While the practice was burgeoning (in the US, more people were utilizing it to relieve their own gender dysphoria), it was in fact almost seventy years old. In 1931, Dora Richter became the first known transgender woman to undergo vaginoplasty surgery, under sex-research pioneer Magnus Hirschfeld at Berlin's Institute for Sexual Research. Or was it Lili Elbe, subject of the film and fictionalized story of her life, *The Danish Girl*, having undergone some of the first surgeries we still use today? Either way, the 1990s thought these surgeries were weird and altogether fascinating (I wonder what the 1930s thought).[3]

I, on the other hand, had discovered a solution to my problem. The problem that arises for any young boy who wants to grow into a woman: you *can't* have a penis and *should* have a vagina.

One surgery to take care of both!

Watching 20/20, I knew enough to be terrified (that was my penis we're talking about) but was unable to wrap my mind around it any more than that. This was something so far outside the realm of possibility for me. It reminded me of the time I told my mom at three years old that I wanted to be a statue for my job when I grew up, and her confirmation that no, that would in fact not be a good career choice—motorcycle rider, on the other hand, was still on the table.

I didn't know if muttering the words "*I'm transgender*" at therapy on that morning would even mean I would have a surgery like that. But saying those words out loud did seem to be a culmination of a transition of sorts. Starting when I saw that *20/20* special.

Until that thirty-fourth birthday dinner, I had been transitioning in the dark. Wondering, waiting, not understanding, never believing it could happen. Learning that gender transition is more than gender affirmation surgery but can include hormones, rewiring your brain, and expressing yourself and moving through the world differently. Transition in the dark included but was not limited to cycles of buying and purging women's clothing; daydreaming about an infinitely impossible reality; finding other people through books, the internet, even *20/20* that seemed to be like me; and blindly stumbling through life, trying to

3 A great article on Dora Richter, called "Remembering Dora Richter, One of the First Women to Receive Gender-Affirming Surgery" by Samantha Riedel (March 15, 2022), can be found online at www.them.us.

avoid any deeper examination of my feelings on the topic. Transition in the dark also included everything else. My life. My being. Constantly in flux and playing a never-ending game of hide-and-seek with myself. Never with an understanding or even a hope that there was anything but darkness.

My transition in the dark continued until the day before that fateful birthday dinner, where light finally shined in. Just days before my thirty-fourth birthday, the darkness was the strongest it had ever been. I was attending a conference two hours away from home and was in another cycle of buying women's clothing, expressing the gender that was inside me, then throwing the clothes out after being so ashamed to look at them. I thought this time was another one of those cycles. As I prepared for two days away from home, I stopped at a Goodwill along my route (an hour away from home because, obviously). Instead of my usual frugality getting the better of me (why buy more than a couple of things when I knew I was going to throw them out?), I spent fifty dollars. At Goodwill. I ended up with everything from dresses to tops to shoes. I'd never splurged on clothing like this before. As I continued to drive, my mind started to wander. I had just spent more money than I ever had on outfits, so maybe I should go all out. I had never bought full outfits: wigs, makeup, other accents like clip-on earrings (in my mid-thirties my mom would still be mad if I pierced my ears).

With this thought nagging away at me, I made a dinner stop at Walmart to get the requisite grapes as well as some not-so-healthy snacks I liked to keep in my hotel room; I decided to see what I could stealthily find, knowing I would have to shop in constant fear of discovery, in a city two and a half hours away from my own. It was to my unending joy that I walked into a Walmart that was ready for Halloween!

No one cared that I really went all out, walking out of there with forty dollars of fake jewelry, wigs, and makeup from the Halloween department. No one whispered "*sick bastard*" under their breath (I was pretty sure this was what was going to happen since I was pretty sure it was what happened any time I bought clothes made for women). I didn't have to make up an excuse: "Uh yeah, my wife is really gonna like this stuff . . ." or "If only I didn't have so many daughters."

None of that. Because it was Halloween, you could let your weirdo wand wave, and no one would bat an eye. And at that point in my life, that's what I thought I was. A weirdo. Someone who felt compelled to do something beyond what society considered normal. A cross-dresser, expressing myself through clothing. A religious sinner. A sinner discovering an ever-widening circle of companion sinners, but a sinner nonetheless.

I went to bed that night, happy to wait for the following evening when, in my hotel room, I would become the woman I always dreamed of being. After my day at the conference, of course.

The next day presented an unexpected wrinkle. I ran into a college professor at the conference. We (he) decided we should get together for dinner, or at least hang out and chat. I really did want to catch up, but not now! Not tonight! I had other plans! I suggested we meet up before dinner, catch up, and then I'd go back to my room to work. Which I did do, among other things.

I went to my room that night and performed the same ritual I had performed many times before. I knew what would happen. I would put on clothes that weren't made to fit my body, feel like I was whole for just a brief moment, then realize they were just clothes and nothing more. I would get angry at myself, feel depressed, shameful, and worthless, and start the same cycle over again.

That night was different though. Putting on these clothes, feeling the full effect of everything else, something inside me unlocked. These were just clothes after all, but with everything put together, I suddenly saw a part of myself. I saw my wholeness for a moment, even though it was clouded by the Goodwill clothes that didn't fit right and the Halloween costume jewelry. I understood I would still throw these things out, hoping never to do this again, but this time, I knew something was different. I didn't know what yet, but I was terrified and simultaneously couldn't wait to find out. No more than forty-eight hours later, my wife gave me that birthday gift, and that night, I started my transition over, in the light, letting Katie in on my burgeoning identity.

It's funny how sometimes shining a light on something, sharing it with someone, is scarier than seeing it in the dark. The light flipped on during that birthday dinner, but it left me with more questions than answers. *What is happening to me? What if I am more than a gender expression bender? What if I'm transgender? What if I'm gay? If I'm transgender, what does gay even mean? Could I be a woman and be straight? What would that mean?*

And that was in the first ten seconds.

For the next two years, I asked questions and explored. I had to figure out who I was. I went to Hamburger Mary's. I talked to friends, I found community online, and I went to therapy. It was finally that day at therapy when the floodlight turned on and wiped most of my questions away.

I was transgender. I now knew too much and there was no going back. Now I wondered what would become of my marriage, my family, my very existence. My transition was now in the bright light, out in the open. The thirty-four years of darkness was a distant memory, and the last two years of transitioning in the light felt like a foundation for something much bigger now.

Yes, transition in the light was much scarier, much more fraught with hazards and so many questions. Transition in the light, out in the open, as I found out very quickly, typically comes with choices to be made. Any transition, whether you're moving from one city to another (where should we live?), graduating from high school (should I go to college; if so, where?), or contemplating changing genders (say what?): it all comes with choices you don't have answers to at the time you make them.

I do not use this term lightly. The word *choices* connotes that I wasn't born with this inside me, that it was some external choice to be made, based on what religion I was born into or the city where I live. That is not what I mean. Choices for me meant I had to act toward an option to try to see myself more clearly.

For me it was Option 1, status quo, or Option 2, everything changes. For Option 1, even though that meant expressing my feminine gender through clothing occasionally, my life would be "normal" by all accounts. I would work to be the best father, husband, son, brother, etc. that I could be, and no one would be the wiser about my hidden transgender identity. This also meant hiding. Not only from others but hiding from myself. I knew it meant that I would feel the crushing weight of that hiding, dying each day under the load of shame that bore down on me, day in and day out, until I breathed my last. I knew Option 1. I was already living it. But then the alternative. Option 2? Who the hell knew? I come home, tell my wife I'm transgender—then what?

After weighing those two options though, it seemed like a no-brainer, I had to tell Katie what I discovered about myself in therapy that day and what I had been slowly discovering through my experiences, like those at my birthday dinner and at the conference—my whole life.

As I drove home on the interstate that loops around the city and through the Iowa countryside, I devised a plan. I would test the waters first. This was something I was wholly used to, dipping a toe in to check for temperature, check for external approval, avoid conflict. "What do you think of me buying these women's jeans, they really look good on me." "How would you feel if I grew my hair out—no reason." That's what I would do with this. Say something like, "So, you know all this stuff we've been talking about? I talked to my therapist today and she mentioned there's a slight chance I might be transgender. I'm not so sure, but she seems to think so. How does that sit with you?"

It was all I could do to not call her on the phone from the car and ask her this question. My anxiety was starting to skyrocket, and I just wanted to get through the conversation. But I had to do this in person.

It wouldn't be fair to Katie if I didn't. I would walk in the door and I would test the waters, then push deeper.

On the remainder of the thirty-minute drive, however, I had a revelation: If I approached this conversation with my half questions, I was manipulating her response. Even if she gave me a good response ("Okay, what do we do now?" was the best I had hoped for), it wouldn't be a real one because I had manipulated it. I wouldn't be giving her the full me. I knew now that I was transgender. Fully transgender. Not a little, but all the way. Whatever that would come to mean. Yes, I was someone who liked to express their feminine side through clothing, but my transgender identity went much deeper than that.

I pulled up to the house and took a breath. I walked in the door, my head full of thoughts, but of course was greeted by my youngest who had been waiting for me to get home.

"Daddy!" he called as he ran and leaped into my arms.

Okay, I had to wait.

I waited through the evening until the kids went to bed before I told Katie I had something to tell her. It was the first time in my life I was scared for us. Our relationship was always the thing I could count on, even during the worst of storms. Where most couples might take out their frustration and emotions on each other during the stressful events we had experienced (miscarriage, adoption stress, financial issues), we never did. They always brought us closer. This one, though, was different. I was changing the game. We had made vows to each other. She said yes to "taking this man, to have and to hold, as long as we both shall live." Until that point, I had always lived up to those vows. I was everything a straight woman could ever want. I was a loving, caring, empathetic, kind, generous, thoughtful, sensitive, and list of wonderful qualities ad nauseam, man. And I was prepared to continue to be all those things except one. That last one was just one little word. By changing that one little word, it could change everything. I had no idea how it would end.

We moved to the kitchen table, and I sat her down. Ever since we had become best friends back in eighth grade, our relationship had been built on a foundation of trust. We had never been people who would beat around the bush with one another, especially when it came to big conversations. So I got to the point.

"I had therapy today and I realized—I'm transgender."

In that one second, it felt like a huge weight was lifted off me. I didn't know how she would respond, and there very well could have been a bomb hanging over my head, but I didn't care. I was free. I didn't realize freedom could rush into my body like this. I had spent my whole life in chains, hiding from myself and others, and speaking my identity out loud to someone I cared about instantly gave me a freedom I had never experienced before, even with everything hanging in the balance. Transition out in the open.

Without missing a beat, she responded, "I know."

Relief washed over my body and I exhaled. Staying in the moment and as we often do in our relationship, I playfully accused her of withholding this information from me. And how long had she known? Almost two years. Ever since that birthday dinner.

Choice number 1: be honest with your wife or manipulate her into giving you an answer you want to hear. I chose to be honest. Check. What's next? Turns out a lot.

Again, I was faced with options. Do I come out to the world or stay closeted or something in between?

Through many more individual therapy sessions and boatloads of long conversations with Katie, I chose to move forward with gender transition supported by a writing exercise my therapist suggested. She asked me to project a life where the status quo reigned. Living as I was then, living in the closet, life as it was, all the way to death. Then project a life where I move toward gender transition, life out in the open, life unknown, life as it would be, all the way to death:

Life as it is

Life as it is and would continue to be if it was as it is, is comfortable. There is privilege. There is margin when it comes to my interactions with society (read: no judgment). My kids are easy to raise; there are hard conversations but never anything out of the ordinary. My kids grow up with a mom and dad. The proverbial "best-case scenario." I continue the status quo in relationships and continue to build new ones. I continue to hide a part of me from everyone I meet, which feels sad. People will know me for my love of people and won't define me primarily by my gender. I get to express myself through style. I get to express my thoughts and feelings and emotions freely, as freely as I can for hiding my true identity, but I am continually frustrated that I've come to a wall I can't get over. I continue to push forward, helping people find their passions and be free, which eventually starts to feel a little disingenuous. I cross into my forties, coach my kids' little league teams, doing all the things good dads are supposed to do. I turn fifty, watching them graduate, wondering if I've limited my world to a much smaller world than is reality with the choices I've made. I think now may be a good time to live "life out loud," but I've come this far and life is good. I retire and travel more, opening myself up to a bigger world. I again think about what could/would be, as the world is a more accepting place, but I am this person now. Both free and chained. I die an old man, having lived a full life, with a nagging regret, sad for what could have been, but grateful and joyful.

Life as it would be

Life as it would be is unknown. It's not something that is easily pictured and thought out. It's a place I'm scared to imagine. It's a place where privilege is gone. It's a place where hate and judgment are drastically increased. My kids have to answer tough questions and may be exposed to ridicule, but they know what love is. They know what *freedom looks like. I expose my true self to everyone. I have nothing to hide. I become more effective in helping people find and live into their passions, although the audience looks a lot different. People identify me as a gender, which is often seen as my most significant trait. I am still a beloved soul, created by God, my true identity, but it can sometimes be overshadowed by my gender. I cross into my forties, embraced by some and ridiculed by others. I start a controversy by wanting to coach my kids' little league teams. My kids have two moms and that is something that defines who they are. I can still teach them to fish, shave, ride a bike, play video games, and be who I am with them. I turn fifty and watch them graduate, wondering if they would be different people had I not made the choice I did. I retire and my experiences lead me to more writing and speaking. I travel with my wife, but it involves meeting with others and helping people find out who they are. My world is open. I am open. My soul is free. I die, an old woman, having lived a full life, understanding pure love and suffering. I wonder if I limited myself by the choices I made (adoption, church leadership, relationships). I know God loves me and I know Love so intimately, in part because of the amazing relationships I have made along the way.*

After putting this on paper, it seemed like a clear choice. I could continue to be who I had chosen to be up to that point, a thirty-something-year-old man with five kids, a wife who was amazing, and an awesome life, or I could choose a new path. I could choose to be what I had really been all along, a woman. Hopefully still with five kids, a wife who is amazing, and an awesome life.

Only time would tell. That's the thing about transitions, they don't work out outside of time. We can't skip from one frame to the next, time traveling through life without experiencing it all. The good, the bad, the euphoria, and the dysphoria have to all be there in order to experience life. And since we can't time travel, it means we're always in transition.

Always a little scared, hoping for the best, planning for the worst. Sometimes seeing far enough down the road to only take the next step. Sometimes wondering how we're still upright when there seems to be no ground beneath us. In liminal space, in transition, throughout all of our lives.

The F-Word

It was a breezy afternoon and my little league team was having a good showing. I, on the other hand, was not. At age twelve, I wasn't the worst kid, but I wasn't the best. Like most things in my life, I was middling. I was good enough to play second base, until I got inside my head over-thinking things and started making errors. Then I was moved to the dreaded *right field*. The place where big league dreams and little league careers go to die. Everyone always felt sorry for the kid in right field. It was always the same.

"Put Jeffrey in right field. No one ever hits the ball out there."

So, there I found myself on a lovely afternoon, already down in the mouth knowing I surely was going to hell because I had masturbated that morning. When I made my second error in the same inning, the pressure started to build. Mom and Dad were in the stands, always supporting me, but I was hardest on myself. After the first error, I shook it off. Surely I missed this ridiculously easy pop fly because of the sun/ wind/moon? But the second one, well, there was no excuse for that. A grounder to the outfield.

In little league, they teach you that when a grounder comes to the outfield, *stay in front of the ball by any means necessary.* Like seriously lie down if you have to. Somehow though, I bent over and it went right through my legs. After frantically chasing it down, making the way-too-long-throw-for-a-kid from the back fence of the outfield to the kid standing way too far out in the outfield because he knew my arm was terribly weak, I thought, *Dang it. I should have had that one.*

Even though I had only thought it and hadn't said it, to me it was the first time I "swore," since I was around five years old. Looking back, I honestly wish I had really taken advantage of it when I was little. Had I known at five that I was going to be punished the way I was, I'd have said *fuck*, or at least *shit*. But I'm fairly certain I got my mouth washed out with soap for saying *crap*. I say fairly certain because it may have been another one of the forbidden "curse" words such as *fart*, *shoot*, or the always dangerous *what the heck*.

It really only took that one time though. Having to chew on a bar of Irish Spring will really make you think twice the next time you want to let the *dang-its* fly. I had gone the past seven years without a swear to that day in little league. But just like that, the *dang-it* was back. My sense memory overwhelmed me as my body shuddered from the thought of a soapy mouth, even though I had only thought about swearing.

Surely thinking *dang-it* was not going to send me straight to hell. I mean, thinking a pseudo-swear was twice removed from saying an actual swear. Maybe it would be a winding road through the foothills of purgatory before arriving at the pearly gates, but surely not hell.

But then it happened.

No one hits the ball to right field, they said.

If they do, it's only once a game, they said.

Three times in one inning? Impossible.

Oh, unless the batter is really good. Then they can hit the ball wherever they want.

And they choose to pick on the poor kid in right field, whoever that may be. The kid picking their nose, pants three sizes too big, hat pulled down crooked over their eyes. These dangerous hitters aren't stupid. They're brilliant.

The ball was hit in between right and center field. I got a great jump on it as I screamed over toward what surely would be a hit. The problem was, I got *too* good of a jump on the ball, motivated by my recent failures. I overran it and had to reach back for it. Clearly this wasn't my day. The impossible catch turned into the easiest catch of the day and then turned into my eternal shame. After I picked the ball up off the grass and tried to throw out the runner who was now rounding second and heading for third, I let another curse fly. This time it was a real, adult curse, out loud.

"Damn it."

Okay, fly might not be the right description, as I said it so fast, in a whisper under my breath, that it could barely be called a spoken word. I was sure that the faster and quieter you got it out, the less it counted on the scoresheet for things that sent you to hell.

I honestly still feel bad for even discussing it. These scripts are deep down inside me somewhere trying to claw their way out. The scripts that produce guilt and shame, ever present companions of the past, seemingly vanquished for moments of true serenity where I can know my true self, only to pop back up when I least suspect them.

Don't do it!
Your family would be so ashamed!
You're going to go to hell, you know.
You can't say curse words out loud, let alone write them down for everyone to see!
You're a seriously unholy person.
Doesn't the Bible say, "Let no unwholesome talk come out of your mouth?"

Damn. Even writing that hurts. Not the *damn*, but the verse from the Bible. Always to shame and condemn me, and not just for *speaking* my words but also for *thinking* my words.

Growing up, I understood the Bible to be my all-encompassing rule book for life and something that contained no less than, it seemed, seventeen thousand ways to tell me how bad I was, or how I missed the mark, or to remind me that I must be perfect to be considered worthy. It also served to remind me that if I missed the mark, I'd come home one day to a pile of folded clothes, left behind because I was a sinner. A few classics include:

"Blessed are those whose ways are blameless, who walk according to the law of the LORD!" (Psalm 119:1)

"Do everything without grumbling or arguing, so that you may become blameless and pure, 'children of God without fault in a warped and crooked generation.'" (Philippians 2:14–15)

"For the flesh desires what is contrary to the Spirit, and the Spirit what is contrary to the flesh. They are in conflict with each other, so that you are not to do whatever you want." (Galatians 5:17)

"Do not let unwholesome talk come out of your mouths." (Ephesians 4:29)

Blameless? All things without grumbling? Aren't I made of flesh? And *what the heck* does unwholesome mean? *Shoot! Crap!*

I want to pause for a minute as I am not trying to cast the Bible in a bad light here. I now understand it to be something much more than a rule book, much broader than literal words on a page, and something much more valuable than the thing that only used to condemn me and never lifted me up. I now appreciate its nuance, its authors' struggles, and the very real truth it contains, teaching us how to love one another and create wider spaces of inclusivity.

But for an ancient wisdom book to be used to make a kid feel shame, to the point that they wonder if they'll ever amount to anything in this world, and to make them certain that they will end up in the fiery pits of hell for eternal torment with the worst, most vile people in the world, all for saying a curse under their breath: that's abhorrent.

And because of that fear instilled inside me, I still remember that first adult curse at the ballfield vividly.

I felt bad. Clearly. I am writing about this now with such vivid memories. The shame sweeping over me now as I sit on my living room couch. It's years later and I'm a mid-thirties, lesbian trans woman who, by all evangelical Christian accounts, should have many more things to be ashamed of than my first *damn-it*. But it still plays. It hangs with me like the boos I'm sure I heard from the other little league dads after making my third error in the same inning. It lies stagnant in my mind, feeling like a permanent stain on my heart. It drops, like a giant F-bomb, obliterating every good thing in its path.

Not that F-bomb though. The one that's even worse.

Failure.

Because failure to adhere to all the rules, failure to be good enough, is simply sin. Many of us were told this. That big F-bomb that would lead to all sorts of places. Failure was really just the edge of the slippery slope to hell. At least that's what they told us.

Worthlessness

"Damn."

The word slipped out in a whisper as I sat on the old worn couch in the corner of my therapist's office. The clock on the wall above my therapist's head, clicking away the seconds of my session, suddenly stopped, as if to taunt me as the walls closed in around me. My world had come unraveled. Not because I cursed, but because of the words I muttered right before that. "I'm transgender."

On the surface, I didn't trust the words I said, but deep in my gut, I knew they were true.

Needing to be able to trust your own emotions and your own body is a theme in the life of many transgender people, including me. And not being able to trust or acknowledge your own emotions and your own body is a theme in the life of many Christians, including me. As someone who now identified both as a Christian and trans, not trusting my emotions and body was clearly a problem.

My therapist, gray and wizened from years of counseling folks to better understand themselves, and from her own push and pull of being an LGBTQ+ Christian, must have seen my panic. The terror written across my face.

"It's okay," she said, as someone who understood from years of this work what was going on inside my body. This was the moment in therapy I had been simultaneously waiting for and hoping would never come.

At first, therapy had been awkward, where we focused on my gender issues and the questions around my gender. To make it worse, during my first few sessions, I had been focusing on my own identity only in the context of others. Then, she started saying things to me like, "Answer that question again, but pretend there is no one judging you for your answer." What this did was help me to understand that the little worth I thought I had built for myself was all contingent on how other people saw me, and none of it was intrinsic to my personhood. Yowch.

Comedian Jerry Seinfeld has a bit where he's talking about Halloween and a small child's reaction to the news that candy is being handed out.

"They're giving out candy? Who's giving out candy? Everyone we know is just GIVING OUT CANDY?!"[4]

That's what I felt like at therapy.

"Wait, what—self-worth? How do I get self-worth? You can have self-worth WITHOUT RELYING ON ANYONE ELSE TO GIVE IT TO YOU?!"

I got glimpses of my newfound discovery in exercises like the one my therapist had me do in preparation for coming out. I wrote out all the things I could think of that defined me other than my gender. There were a few things on that list that smelled like self-worth.

I am good at the core.
I am thoughtful.
I am humorous.
I deserve love.
I am a trusted colleague.
My emotions can be trusted.

But that voice in the background from my evangelical Christian upbringing got louder and louder the closer I got to realizing I could

---

4 Jerry Seinfeld, *Is This Anything?* (Simon and Schuster, 2020)

trust myself. "This is why we told you not to trust therapists. They can't be trusted. You can't trust yourself. You know that. Why would you even want to trust yourself? You're worthless. You'll go to hell if you trust yourself; you know that, right?"

I didn't want to end up on that *slippery slope* to hell, something I learned all about growing up.

Leaders at church told us all about the slippery slope, which was meant to scare us away from small sins, leading us to believe if we couldn't avoid the small sins, we would move toward much bigger sins, such as "Don't kiss your girlfriend because then you'll want to touch each other, and then you'll want to have sex, and then you'll end up pregnant." A slippery slope from kissing to being a parent at age sixteen. Or "Don't listen to rock music because those lyrics will get in your head. You will think about them and dwell on them, and then you'll start to hang out with the wrong crowd, start to do crime, and eventually if you do these things enough, demons will inhabit your soul."

Each slippery slope metaphor was full of half-truths and major consequences. But if we did exactly as we were told, followed all the rules, we would be fine.

There were many rules, gates that kept you from going down that slope. They came from church, they came from the Christian school I attended, and they came from my parents. Most of them were *don't* rules, with a few *dos* sprinkled in for good measure.

Don't curse.
Don't lie.
Don't cheat.

Okay, these aren't so bad.

Don't gossip.
Don't be mean.
Don't hate others.

Okay, I can do this!

Don't masturbate.
Don't have a desire to have sex.
Do read your Bible every day.
Do pray without ceasing.

Uh oh.

Do put God first.
Do put yourself last (self-flagellate).
Don't think you know anything.
Do think your parents and authority figures and the church know everything.
Don't trust yourself.
Don't have emotions.

Oh dear, I'm toast.

I didn't realize how much those last two, *don't trust yourself* and *don't have emotions*, were ingrained inside me. Deep, deep ruts—so deep they seemed like they were permanent structures until I went to therapy.

I remember when I came out to my parents, the first thing they did was thank me. They told me that by bringing my sin into the light, we could take care of it together—by sending me to a Christian therapist. And by Christian therapist, I mean a paraprofessional in the church who has no license to practice mental health therapy whatsoever. These folks were common in the evangelical church where I was raised and where the science behind emotions and mental health tended to be ignored. Actual licensed and experienced therapists (especially if not Christian) were understood to be the direct spawn of Satan. They were expert manipulators who would purport to be bearers of light but could direct the unaware subject down a path to certain destruction faster than you can say, "Tell me about your relationship with your mother."

Before coming out to my parents, I had found an actual therapist, who happened to be Christian, yet who also helped me realize that there was no sin that needed to come to light. What I needed to understand was my worth.

Once I started to realize that my own worth was buried at the bottom of that slippery slope, it started to come together. To get to it though, I had to get through all the bullshit the church had piled onto it. I had to get underneath it all to my essence.

After my first therapist helped me realize I was transgender with the future projection exercise, my next therapist helped me feel again. She helped me get beneath the worthlessness and detachment I brought with me when I sat down on that couch in her office for the first time. I went to therapy and I had to dig. Oh, did I dig. I had to remember and think and sort through my expressive charismatic upbringing. She helped me reexperience my past experiences in both mind and body through EMDR therapy, a hallmark of my sessions with her.[5] I had to dig through all the scripture repetition that, looking back, was designed to bury emotions and self-perception until I no longer existed through my own will, and instead I was only the layers of religion that surrounded me. In fact, I now understand that my descent on the slippery slope wasn't because I fell and slid down. I actually couldn't get past the gates that led down to the slope. They were locked tight, so instead I dug down. Some would say I've dug all the way to the bottom, the place where the devil himself resides. I would say it's simply a place where I can feel. I can now move from my head to my body and really feel. This theme of feeling my emotions keeps coming up because when you feel for the first time after years of not feeling, it's jarring. It needs to be processed.

---

5 Eye movement desensitization and reprocessing (EMDR) is a type of psychotherapy that helps people process traumatic memories and other distressing experiences, theorizing that traumatic memories leave open loops in the brain that need to be reprocessed and closed. It can be used for quite small as well as large traumatic events.

Once I started to feel, I realized very quickly that self-worth wasn't just going to spring to life and help me understand who I was. It was a heavy burden that couldn't be unloaded in one therapy session. A notion and feeling of worthlessness is a burden I have carried since I was a small child, and it crushed every part of me.

From the earliest age, I can remember wanting so badly to pass the test as a Christian but knowing I never could (at least that's what I was told). I remember every year at church camp, we would sing and worship, knowing we weren't holy and needed help.[6] We'd wonder how we could be holy, but then someone would authoritatively state the answer! We needed to go home and burn all our secular CDs. What? Noooooo! I had just discovered Columbia House and the magic of the one cent CD (just make sure to cancel your subscription)! But I wanted to be holy, so I came home from church camp, broke all my CDs that had any curse words in them, and sold the rest to Sam Goody. I still have a twinge of guilt for keeping my Matchbox Twenty CD.

Every year I tried to be a better Christian and was told to keep trying, because to give up trying meant that I *really wouldn't* get it right, and the consequences of that were much more dire than trying to get it right and failing. This burden of trying to meet expectations, over and over and over, weighed me down and tried to suffocate me. It felt like a sick carnival game. The carney telling me I *had* to spend the money to try again, with the prize being a giant stuffed animal, though this one was behind a curtain. Each time I would win, the carney would say, "Sorry, kid, that's just the small one, try again!" The problem was, I couldn't leave the carnival. I couldn't opt out because all life was this twisted carnival. Failing over and over, and even when I didn't fail, I was told, "You are so worthless that God had to kill his son to save you." Through it all, I soon figured out that I didn't matter. Not *life* didn't

6   For a quick primer on what a charismatic upbringing looks like, watch the film *Jesus Camp.*

matter, but *I* didn't matter. A meaninglessness that still rears its head from time to time.

Through this burden of self-flagellation and self-hatred, I came to inhabit worthlessness. And during those times when preachers and teachers would encourage me to forget about this life and live "in light of eternity," to look at the big picture, take the long view, back all the way out . . . it got even more depressing.

I remember an image they would teach at our Christian school to convey the concept of eternity. They would tell our fifth grade, yo-yo-playing-at-recess minds metaphors like this:

Imagine the earth, the size it is now, but it is made of brass.

And imagine a dove flies by the earth, every thousand years, and brushes the earth with its wings, ever so gently.

Now imagine when that brass ball the size of the earth is ground into dust . . .

That is the beginning of eternity.

The metaphor was meant to cement in us that failure was not an option, especially in light of eternity which is really, really—really long.

Stepping back, I realize now that I can attribute most of my feelings of worthlessness to religion. But religion isn't a thing in and of itself. It takes people to be the face of a religion and make things happen. And when good people, like parents, teachers, preachers, or friends, are told they're worthless, deserving of the worst hell imaginable, they can't help but pass that along to others in order to save souls.

Looking back, it was obvious.

I should back up though. I did have a delightful childhood (you may be wondering at this point if I have a serious propensity for truth stretching).

My parents were great. They loved me, they gave me everything I needed, they didn't really make me do a ton of stuff I didn't want to (aside from the occasional trumpet lesson or daily devotional session), but it didn't matter.

A community that incorporates systemic worthlessness overpowers even the most charmed, privileged daily life, wrestling away the thing that it needs most, unconditional love, replacing it with shame.

On some level, by the way I felt inside and how I responded to the world around me, I knew that I was transgender growing up. But when I was young, even into my teens and early twenties when I was expressing my gender more, knowing myself fully beneath the pile of worthlessness and shame was more out of reach than I could have possibly realized.

As a kid and young adult, I felt like I didn't matter, so why even get to know who I was? I knew what was inside me, or so I thought. I didn't really want to find out what it was and what other vile things lay beneath the surface. So I stuck to my outside, cleaning my surface, which stayed clean like a fresh pair of white New Balances in a freshly blacktopped world. If I dug beneath, it could get ugly.

So, I was content. Content to know that I didn't really know the full story of myself. Letting worthlessness drive the car to keep me hidden. It was a car, though, that I tried to upgrade every few years as I'd learn about a new personality trait that helped me in life, like how to be a good listener. (Turns out you can listen well when you're avoiding talking about yourself.)

I learned recently after thirty years of playing the game Chutes and Ladders (originally Snakes and Ladders), that it is a Hindu game of virtue and Karma. Two steps forward in life, one step back. And I now understand why I, like most who play the game, liked the chutes better than the ladders, even when the goal is to get to the top. Perfection is hard, and we can learn so much about ourselves from the slide down the slippery slope.

As I discovered more of myself, I no longer wanted to be perfect and get to the top. I slowly was desiring to get to the bottom of myself.

And in doing so, I realized that worthlessness was the overarching theme of my life. For most of us, worthlessness can't exist in a small corner of our being. Instead, it's something that gets into our small cracks and crevices and spreads. Like water, it fills up our empty spaces. And when we don't know ourselves, especially in the case of someone like me, there are a lot of empty spaces to fill up.

Realizing I had a problem with feeling like I was worthless was just the beginning though. To keep moving forward, I had to go through the shame.

Coming Out

I sat at my desk, clock ticking down to 5:00 p.m. when I would finally be able to leave work. It's not that I didn't love my work as a human resources director, I did. But being cooped up in an office on a perfect fall afternoon was practically criminal. It was a balmy sixty-eight degrees in Iowa but the air was crisp. That day had been tiring with emergency after emergency (everything's an emergency in HR), and I decided to take a break around 4:00 p.m. I looked down at my phone, and there were some social media notifications. As I clicked to see what was going on, I realized the sitting president had done something to roll back protections for transgender individuals. The headlines read something like this one from the *New York Times*:

> "'Transgender' Could Be Defined Out of Existence Under the Trump Administration."

The article went on to describe how "the [first] Trump administration [was] considering narrowly defining gender as a biological, immutable condition determined by genitalia at birth, the most drastic move yet in a government wide effort to roll back recognition and protections of transgender people under federal civil rights law."[7]

In essence, the president wanted to change the stance of the federal government so that gender was the same thing as biological sex and was

---

7   Erica L. Green, Katie Benner, and Robert Pear, "'Transgender' Could Be Defined Out of Existence Under Trump Administration," *The New York Times*, October 21, 2018, https://www.nytimes.com/2018/10/21/us/politics/transgender-trump-administration-sex-definition.html.

trying to eliminate gender protections for millions of transgender people.

I knew I was transgender, but at that moment, because I wasn't out (and wasn't planning to come out anytime soon), I wasn't affected by any move to restrict civil rights. However, many of my friends would be. I got online to post about it (from my perspective as a perceived straight white male), to be angry on behalf of my out trans friends, but I just couldn't do it. Something inside me was more connected to this than simply being angry for my friends. I got angry and frustrated that I couldn't say anything to my family and friends about this from the perspective of a transgender woman, because no one knew I was a transgender woman.

Emboldened by my feelings over the move by Trump, I felt it was time to let my family know. As someone who had always felt supported by my family, I just knew that if any of them, specifically my parents, knew I was transgender, they'd go, "Oh, we didn't know! We change our minds about trans people! We want the best for our child; this news is horrible!!!" This moment of unbridled hope provided the courage, paired with wild adrenaline that obfuscated and undervalued the facts of my religious upbringing, for me to send a letter to parents, siblings, and in-laws.

It read:

So, I don't really want to send this to you in an email, but I can't wait any longer. What the Trump administration is doing to transgender people is abominable, and I can't stand by idly anymore. I need to speak out. I watch online today as many of my transgender friends are waiting to be marginalized by the Trump administration and can't sit quietly anymore. The only problem is, I can't speak out how I want to speak out, because I'm not out. You see, I'm a transgender person. I wanted you to know. Not many people know, and I have attached a letter that I wrote for you, and fumblingly send it to you to read. I'm sure much discussion will follow. I love you and look forward to talking with you about this. Anytime you're available to come over to our house or sit down, I'd love to do that. You can call as well.

That night I waited for something, anything by way of response from all of them. My adrenaline had subsided, and I knew I was beyond a point of no return. The undo send button on my email was no longer an option. My sister-in-law emailed me first to let me know she loved me and cared for me and was glad I had decided to share myself fully with her. My dad then emailed, saying he didn't understand but loved me and wanted to talk more even though he felt we would disagree. My mom then called to say she loved me and we would talk more later. My sister sent me a text saying it was brave for me to come out and she'd call later.

Okay, not terrible reactions. Much better than I hoped for. Little did I know that everyone was holding back how they really felt.

The following day felt different. Something *was* different. Even though my internal emotions were high, it felt as if the pressure valve had been released. A huge weight had been lifted, replaced by a smaller one of relationships in the balance. I got a text from Mom early asking if she could "come out to see me" at work in the morning. I said sure and we set up a time. She arrived at my work before I did, and she asked that I come out to see her rather than her coming in. I obliged and came out and got in her car. She proceeded to hug me and say she loved me, then drove me out of the parking lot of my workplace to a parking lot across the street (this should have been a warning sign) where she proceeded to tell me how she really felt. We talked for forty-five minutes about theology, the crux of the issue. She told me I was giving God the middle finger and that if I proceeded, this would be the most selfish thing I've ever done in my whole life.

Through the course of this conversation, I came to the abrupt conclusion that we serve different Gods. She saw a God waiting to send wrath. A God who can't be in the presence of sin. I told her I see a God, through Jesus who shows us God's true nature, who loves and says, "This is me." She told me she loved me and drove me back to work.

That morning, I also met with my brother to discuss a client for a business we were running together at the time. We hugged awkwardly and went into our meeting. Afterward, we went to lunch, where he was at a loss to find words and wrap his mind around it. I could see it. I let him ask questions and tried to answer them, but we parted, and I knew he was struggling as most do when someone they love comes out as transgender.

Late that afternoon, I got a phone message from my brother-in-law. The first thing he told me was that I was courageous and proceeded to give me some advice. He told me to leave town. Me being transgender would affect my parents, he said, and the right thing to do would be to leave, to move. A weird conversation to say the least, but overall, he asked a lot of questions, and it seemed as though the conversation went well.

Three days later, I took the day off work to clean my basement, which was long overdue. Midway through the morning, I got word there was a transgender rights rally going on at our state capitol in response to the president's actions. I spontaneously got dressed and went out in public to the rally, by myself—as myself—for the first time. It was an amazing experience and felt wonderful to be myself in public. The positivity people held amidst hate astounded me, and I remember thinking, *I hope I can reflect that positivity throughout my process of coming out. I hope I can show love in the face of things like this.*

As conversation with my family continued, things started to devolve. My sister was super upset and started telling people that Katie was making me trans, that she was a demon, a heretic, leading me astray (although my sister hadn't even called me yet). She also told people I was sexually abused as a kid, and she thought she knew by who (not true and again, what the hell?). My brother tried to play mediary, stuck in the middle of trying to love multiple people who were in conflict.

That weekend, a week after I had first come out, I sent letters to pastors and some other people at the church where we were leaders. This was the letter:

Family,

I have been a part of your life and you a part of mine since the day I was born. Over that time, you have perceived me a certain way, as we all perceive each other through the lens we have. I hope this letter makes that perception clearer and not cloudier. This is a hard conversation for me to have, but I want you to know me fully.

First, I want to remind you of some things that you may or may not know about me. I am a lover of people. I am passionate about helping others pursue their dreams. I am analytical. I am slow to speak. I am even-keeled and laid-back. I am thoughtful. I am empathetic. I am not judgmental. I am a lover of creation. I am relational. I am humorous. I love color. I love the diversity of creation, including people. I love the outdoors. I love to laugh. I love to push boundaries for others. I love to grow. I am a writer. I am passionate about my work because it's relational. I am a helper. I am a peacemaker (Enneagram 9 with an 8, challenger wing so I can get fiery). I am a child. I am a parent. I am a sibling. I am a trusted colleague. I am a spouse. I am body, mind, and spirit.

Some of those things may or may not surprise you, but I wanted you to know that those are some of the things that define who I am. These aren't all the things that define me, but some of the things that define me at my core. My relationship with you has been defined over time, in a familial context. That's one of the things that makes this the scariest and most difficult thing I've ever had to communicate to you. I am a transgender individual.

Since early in my life, I've understood myself to be different. Not understanding why people couldn't relate to me as a girl/woman when I was younger. As I've grown, I've realized this is no one's fault, but I am perceived how people see me, as a male. Sometimes people who experience their own gender differently than the world perceives it, as I do, struggle with depression their whole life, including tendencies toward suicide. This is not the case for me. I have enjoyed my life up to this point and have never felt severely depressed about not being my true gender to the point of suicide like many people.

For me, I have always hoped people would relate to me as a woman because that's how I relate to myself. I don't hate being a man, it just doesn't fully fit who I am. I am not fully me. This is the one thing about my life that I have hidden. I try to be vulnerable with people, and my intent was not to deceive, but this is something that I have been conditioned to be ashamed of and hide. As I have made myself known to people, the shame and guilt has slowly fallen away, thanks to the grace of God.

I'm sure this brings up a ton of questions, and I'll try to answer a few. First, Katie and I are awesome, and in this together. I will always be there for her (as she has been there for me through my life leading up to this point and now) and work together with her to guide our kids in life. She is the love of my life and that hasn't changed. I know this may feel like something out of left field to you but to me, it's me revealing who you already know in the fullest. Second, you may wonder about transition. This is a hard question for me to answer, and most people who I've told have jumped to what they think is the logical end: a full transition to be a woman. That may or may not happen with me. I am on a journey, and I don't want to lead anyone on one way or another of what may or may not happen. What I can say is that I'm taking this one step at a time, with people around me to help me process along the way. I am thinking about everything. And I'll keep moving forward until I feel like I shouldn't anymore. That may take me to a full transition (whatever that means) and that may not. I know that's not much of an answer, but it's where I am right now.

This is not something I can keep hidden anymore, and with the help of my therapist and those who love me, I have understood that *being fully myself in life is more important for my health and well-being, and more important for my relationships that are built on trust and authenticity, than keeping this hidden.*

Transgender is an umbrella term and means different things to different people. I would encourage you to drop any preconceptions that you have about the word and about transgender people and just ask me. My experience is different, and I am telling you this so you know me fully, so if you read things online, understand that my experience may or may not line up, so know you don't have to fill in your own gaps, but you can just ask me. I am very open to talking about my experience up to this point. This goes beyond outward expression. However, clothes are an easy way of outward expression and will help people to relate to me as the woman I've always seen myself as.

Telling you this is very scary to do. I don't know how you will react. Will you accept me, disassociate with me, condemn me, or preach to me? All I know is, at this point in my life, I have to be me.

I understand how your perception of me and our relationship might change, but I hope it changes for the better. I am sad that I've had to keep this from you for so long and that you may feel like you haven't known the full me (although I feel you have, you've just been missing this important link). I love you and will always be your family.

I hit send on this email to my wider community, then waited.

The weeks that followed entailed more painful conversations, where it didn't seem like anyone was listening to a word I was saying. Even with my invitation to ask questions, no one asked any about who I was. No one wanted to know how I felt or how I had lived with this my whole life. No one seemed to care about me in the middle of this, but only about how it affected them.

Not one question—only one-dimensional discussions about theology. Eventually, I drew a boundary. I would not debate doctrine with anyone anymore; it wasn't productive. This led to my parents starting to keep their distance, and my sister officially ending our relationship when she found out a few months later that I was going by a different name.

It was hard. The pain and grief of losing family members who are still living is intense. It comes and goes, but there's a constant throbbing pain beneath the surface.

Over a year later, Katie's family started trying to use my new name. It felt like a big step for our relationship. I reentered the relationship as the new, evolving me slowly and hesitantly, afraid to be hurt, but nonetheless they were trying and so was I. A few months after that, I got invited to Christmas by my mom. A wonderful invitation for a child waiting and wanting to be seen by their parents. After the invitation by text, I called her because I wanted to make sure she could honor my new boundary, the only boundary (aside from the theology talk) that I had: please call me by my new name, Nia. When I called, she told me she couldn't do it. And it wasn't the "I really want to, I'll come around, but I just can't right now" couldn't. It was the "I will not succumb to your delusion, you are a product of the devil, I will not change my mind and will take this to my grave" couldn't.

Even though it was probably impossible, I wished that my parents could have gone through my early transition with me. The part where I had to mourn the "loss" of the person of my previous self, the person I had lived with my whole life, the person they knew me to be. I had to grieve myself to move forward. But they didn't want to enter this mourning process and instead withdrew, telling me I had killed the person they knew, and I moved forward without them. They clung to a vision of who they perceived me to be, not listening to who I was telling them I was.

Some advice I would give to parents of kids who are coming out to them: no matter how shocking it is to you, pay attention. Pay attention while your child is in the shallow end, telling you who they are. Pay attention when the tide is low. Enter into the hard conversations. It gets deep fast, and the tide comes in quickly. Before you know it, things have changed, most likely for the better, but if you don't pay attention at the beginning and try to embrace it, you may miss it like my parents did.

I remember that moment talking to my mom, the love draining from my body. Not the love that is at the core of who I am, but a different love. A love I felt as my mother's child. A love that can't exist and must leave when a mother tells her child she can't be in a relationship anymore. A love that runs away in an all-out sprint when a mother berates her child, telling them they are a product of Satan. This love that I thought was ingrained so deep in my body, suddenly and seemingly completely gone.

I never thought it would end like this.

My insides scorched after just one phone call, creating an acute grief in a way I've never felt before. I cried myself to sleep that night, wondering if I would ever feel anything in the way of a mother's love ever again. I woke up the next morning with the same lingering question sitting in the pit of my stomach, keenly aware that no surrogate will ever take the place of a mother's love.

I asked to be called by my name, Nia, but she couldn't do it. She can't acknowledge me as a daughter and nothing I could do could ever make me a woman, she said. I wish I could plead and beg for her to stay, to love me, to see me, but I can't. I know I can't live in that world any longer because I am not a man and never was.

When she told me on the phone that I'll never be a woman, I wish I would have had the clarity of mind to respond with "I already am." I'm not a cis woman, or a Black woman, or a blue-eyed woman, or a petite woman, or any other type of woman I'm not or haven't yet become. Even though my mom wants to shadow me with doubts, I know beyond doubt that I am and have always been a transgender woman. I have to move forward, and I hope someday that she and the others who currently aren't in my life any longer will decide to join me. It's not an easy path, but one I choose to stay on because here I'm free.

The Visitation

"What was that?"

I sat up straight in the bed and asked Katie the question.

"I don't know," she said, confirming that she heard it too and that it wasn't my 2:00 a.m. brain fog hearing things.

"It was a crunch, crunch, crunch, knock, knock, knock, and the door handle jiggled, right?"

"Yep. We should probably check it out," Katie replied, implying I should get out of bed.

I slowly moved toward the door of our rented casita. There was a courtyard between the main house and the casita, full of gravel, the kind that would *crunch, crunch, crunch* under someone's shoes if they had walked over it to the casita. I pulled back the curtains but couldn't see much in the dark, the moon lighting up only half of the courtyard. My heart was pounding as I opened the door expecting to be face-to-face with a stranger. Perhaps a polite thief who knocked, knowing they might be able to break in to a house more easily if some idiot opens the door.

As I eased the door open, I was face-to-face with nothing but the cool night air. I took a step out into the courtyard, hoping I could see footprints in the gravel or catch a glimpse of someone leaving, but nothing.

I made my way back inside through the adobe arched door and locked it, running my hands over the lock three times for good measure, pulled the curtains tight, and lay back down in the bed.

"It was nothing," I said, unsure of the next steps.

"Okay," she said, promptly lying back down and going to sleep.

I was alone with my thoughts racing. What was that?

It was March of 2019 when Katie and I decided to attend the Center for Action and Contemplation Conference called "The Universal Christ" in Albuquerque, New Mexico.[8] We were fully embedded in our evangelical faith, and the conference was very progressive, if not a controversial conference for us to go to at the time.

Knowing that Richard Rohr, the conference leader, practiced a brand of inclusive Catholicism that loved and accepted everyone (so controversial, I know), I decided to attend the conference as myself, fully out (not yet fully proud). This simply meant bringing a different set of clothes and going by a different name. At that point, I had come out to family and a few close friends only and wasn't sure where "coming out" would lead.

The day we left for the conference, I had a slight panic about going through airport security with my old name but expressing my female gender identity, but it turned out to be unfounded, as we made it through security with no problems. As we settled onto the plane, I recognized a friend's mom. I knew she'd attended these conferences in the past, and I didn't want to shock and surprise her by having her run into me without any explanation. So, I messaged my friend, got his mom's email, and typed a message quickly before the plane took off, coming out to her in case I bumped into her at the conference (or disembarking the plane). The tone for our trip was set, as coming out in the spur-of-the-moment would be a theme in the next four days.

We arrived in New Mexico and had a couple of days to explore before the conference started. The first night was lovely, and we got to explore old town Albuquerque complete with a fabulous dinner. I should clarify, the food was fabulous. During that dinner, the stress that is

---

8   The Universal Christ Conference was named after a book of the same name by Richard Rohr: *The Universal Christ: How a Forgotten Reality Can Change Everything We See, Hope For, and Believe* (Convergent Books, 2019).

transitioning genders got to both Katie and me. I won't relay the whole conversation, but because we'd had such a lovely day—a day that felt like old times—near the end of the evening, Katie said, "*I just wish things could go back to how they were.*" Oh boy.

What she meant by this was she wished our small family could just be a family again, doing the things families do, without the stress of coming out, without everyone judging us, looking at us, talking about us. Without all the stress that is a gender transition. Before I chose to come out, life was easier. As easy as it could have been for having five kids, one of whom has cerebral palsy, all under the age of ten.

But what I heard was *I wish you could just go back to being a man.*

I feel the need to reiterate, that is not what Katie said or what she meant, only what my brain heard. I heard judgment. I was so used to it from other people at that point. In the previous six months, I had been judged more than I had been judged the entire thirty-six years prior. So naturally I heard judgment.

Before dinner I had been reading Amber Cantorna-Wylde's book *Unashamed: A Coming Out Guide for LGBTQ Christians*, which helped me become aware of just how much shame and judgment I still had for myself.[9] Looking back, I can see how being aware of those feelings of shame and judgment made it easy for me to project them onto my spouse. Surely if I felt ashamed and judged by me, she was ashamed of me and was judging me too.

That night, I couldn't sleep. I tossed and turned and had fever dreams. I felt like crawling out of my skin. For most of my life I had not experienced suicidal ideations like many trans and LGBTQ+ people do, but that night I did. I didn't see a way forward without my world crumbling. I tried to picture in my mind how we could go backward to the time before, but I couldn't. I felt that I failed, and I needed to get out of

---

9   Amber Cantorna-Wylde, *Unashamed: A Coming-Out Guide for LGBTQ Christians* (Westminster John Knox Press, 2019).

an impossible situation. Fortunately, in the midst of this panic brought on by shame, I was able to fall asleep enough to avoid what seemed to be the inevitable consequences of that moment.

The next day, I brought up Katie's remark and told her what had happened the previous night and that I didn't see a way to go back without moving forward. She told me of course she didn't mean she wanted me to be a man, but hoped we could eventually feel like we had before—like a regular family just living a regular life. As much as I appreciated her reassurance, I still didn't see how that could be possible. I didn't see a way forward. Everything was changing. It seemed the ease of life we used to know was a pipe dream and was gone forever, something not found in the world of a transgender person—at least, I couldn't envision it yet. I got dressed, and with our last free morning before the conference, we headed to the Center for Action and Contemplation. We wanted to see what this spiritual community looked like. We wanted to feel the presence of God.

We arrived at the unassuming adobe compound excited to explore, but there wasn't much physical space to explore, which seemed intentional. The exploration would be done inside oneself. So we took our time, going through the bookshop and then out to the prayer labyrinth. If you're not familiar with a prayer labyrinth, do a quick Google search to see what one looks like. Theirs was specifically designed to imitate stages of life. As I walked it, I was so sure I was going the wrong way. So strongly in fact, that I almost had a panic attack and hopped out of it. It was the most intense, visceral feeling of two steps forward, one step back that I've ever experienced. But I stayed the course and got to the center of it, and then proceeded to walk it again to exit.

As I wandered the grounds, I came to the hermitage dedicated to Julian of Norwich, a medieval woman famous for her mystical visions of Jesus. This was a tiny building with an unassuming yard behind it with a small bench. I sat down on that bench in the sun and closed my eyes. I sat there, trying to be present with all my swirling thoughts. If you are the sum of your thoughts, I was a hot garbled mess. As I sat, still in the morning sunshine, a calm came over me. I felt someone sit next to me on the bench and put their arm around my shoulders. I opened my eyes thinking I would see Katie, but no one was there. I closed my eyes again and could still feel a body sitting next to mine, an arm wrapped around me. The calm that coursed through me insisted that I rest my head. So I did. I laid my head on the shoulder of the person sitting next to me. It was a relief. I knew someone was holding me in my darkest moment. And I physically felt that love from the available shoulder on which I could rest my head.

I opened my eyes, feeling content in knowing I was loved for who I am. As someone who isn't prone to mystical experiences regularly, and in fact is ruled by logic (as much as a trans person can be), this was something special for me. I went to find Katie to tell her about my encounter. She had just finished the prayer labyrinth and, feeling the mysticism in that place herself, she understood. She didn't make me feel stupid by telling me it wasn't real, but knew I was on a journey.

We headed over to the conference as planned and ended up meeting some fabulous people that I had to come out to immediately. I felt like maybe a way forward was possible. It was the love of others, without judgment, which allowed me to come to a fork in the road, the crux of this story.

The last day of the conference came quickly, and during one of the last sessions, I felt the strong urge to process some emotions. The conference organizers, understanding this sort of thing may happen at their conferences, had set up a processing/quiet room where people could go to write, read, close their eyes and meditate, or just sleep.

I needed to write. I needed to process. And apparently, I needed to hear something. I closed my eyes and just wrote what I heard. I wrote:

"Let Love overwhelm you. Let my Love overwhelm you. Let who you are in me sink into your soul. You are presence. You are peace.

You are Love. Let the Love you have inside spread to yourself. Let me whisper something to you. You are good and you are right. You are so good, and you are so right."

This was the closest to automatic writing I'd ever experienced. It felt effortless, as if I wasn't the one doing the writing and also as if I had to listen to what was being written.

Okay then.

That afternoon I purchased a sermon on CD by Rohr called "Discharging Your 'Loyal Soldier.'"[10] Although I didn't get a chance to listen to it that day, I had heard Rohr speak about the concept enough that I knew what I needed to do to move forward. I needed to discharge the part of me that had been protecting my soul, the person who was no small part of who I had been, if I wanted to move forward.

Later that evening, I had an intense EMDR session that Katie helped me through.[11] There I was, face-to-face with the person I knew myself as—a male protector. The one who carried all my burdens, including the worthlessness and shame that had built up. I didn't realize how much shame he was carrying to protect me, until I discharged him. I told him his service was no longer needed. Through tears, I thanked him for his service, for the years he had kept me safe from harm. I thanked him for the memories and all the times he had carried the shame and judgment. With all the shame and judgment that was poured onto him, he had done his best not to shame and judge others, but to hold it as his own. I could feel his burden disappear when he turned around and walked away. And with that, my shame lifted in an instant. I wrote in my journal:

---

10 This CD can be purchased at the Center for Action and Contemplation's online store at https://store.cac.org/products.

11 Although EMDR most of the time should be done with a licensed therapist, the founder of the method, Francine Shapiro, has authored a book that walks people through processing on their own. It's called *Getting Past Your Past: Take Control of Your Life with Self-Help Techniques from EMDR Therapy*, (Rodale Books, 2013).

The Fog of shame and guilt has lifted. My Love for me is now revealed. Sprayed with morning Light. Surrounded by all Creation. The Beauty of everything is inherent. Some hidden by Oppression. Others shrouded in Fog. My Beauty is Out. Revealed to me by the Love of others. I am Revealed.

The session with Katie and the journal writing happened over the course of an hour or so. Afterward, my body was spent and I slept. Hard. Until I was awakened by the *crunch, crunch, crunch, knock, knock, knock.*

As I lay there in bed, having determined no one was there, and Katie sound asleep again, I tried to make sense out of the past few days, and to make sense of the footsteps and knocking Katie and I both definitely heard. I became convinced that it was my "loyal soldier" coming back, reporting for duty. Bringing with him all the shame and guilt he always carried. I never told him not to come back after all, so why wouldn't he try to come back to make sure I was protected?

I then had what I'll describe as a waking dream. Or maybe it was a vision or perhaps another EMDR session. I say this because in my EMDR sessions with my therapist, I have spent a lot of time in the backyard of my childhood home. This was my safe space where I could talk to little me and get to know her. In this vision, I was in this same backyard.

Little me was there. Her name is Ant—the small version of my full name, Antonia.

She said to me, "Are you ashamed of me?"

Of course not.

"Why are you ashamed of yourself then? We're the same person," she says.

I tell her we're not. At least, I'm older.

She grows to the size of an adult and is wearing a wedding dress.

She asks again, "Are you ashamed of me now?"

Of course not.

"Are you still ashamed of yourself?" she asks.

Yes. Even though we're the same size, we're different people.

She hugs me and we become the same. I am now her, dressed in the same dress. She tells me to look in the mirror.

I go to the garage where there is a mirror. It's cloudy. I can't see myself. I realize maybe I'm supposed to move. I have a waking thought that maybe it was me who made the footsteps and knocked on the casita door. I head toward my childhood house, hearing the same *crunch, crunch, crunch* under my feet as I walk the gravel path to the basement door. I knock on the door, hearing the same knocks the night visitor made. The handle jiggles and the door opens to reveal my mom. I haven't talked to her in so long, but she hugs me firmly, invites me in, tells me I'm beautiful, and tells me she has a full-length mirror I can use. I go to it and look, but I still can't see myself clearly. It's foggy. We part and I go back outside. I talk to Ant again who is still an adult.

"Are you ashamed of God?" she asks.

Of course not!

She asks, "Do you think God is ashamed of you?"

Yes. I do.

She tells me she is God and she's not ashamed of me. I don't believe her.

She gives me a hug and suddenly I'm her again, I'm God, she's God, she's me. We're all the same, three of us there together. She tells me to go to the mirror again.

I head toward the garage, hesitant in what I might see, but this time the mirror is not foggy and reveals all of me. A beautiful woman is staring back at me. I go back to the yard feeling ecstatic. I tell Ant I'm worried. This is great, but it can't last. I'm dreaming. I'll have to leave.

She asks me to follow her. We go around to the back of the garage where there is a bench. She tells me to sit. I do, and she sits next to me and puts her arm around me. I put my head on her shoulder.

"Do you remember this?" she asks.

Our time together at the Center for Action and Contemplation, where she/myself/God was with me and sat next to me.

"This is possible all the time and in all places," she says to me.

In a moment, I have flashes of all the times I memorized/meditated on the Bible verse in the book of Joshua: "Have I not commanded you? Be strong and courageous. Do not be afraid; do not be discouraged, for the LORD your God will be with you wherever you go."[12]

A "life-verse" that lost meaning long ago, riddled with the context of war and death, suddenly comes to full life.

I understand it wholly. It took me thirty-six years to understand one verse in the Bible.

We walk back to the swing set in the yard, Ant shrinking back to her little six-year-old size.

She says, "Lean down here, let me whisper something into your ear."

I crouch and she says, "Sweet Nia. You are good and you are right. You are so good, and you are so right."

Inhale. Exhale.

As I awoke for the morning, from a fever dream of a night, I felt free. Free from the shame and guilt that bubbled up when Katie made that remark about going back. The freedom felt so good. I knew I couldn't go back. I could finally move forward.

The final day of the conference was excellent. We had dinner with new friends, and I could feel the path forward. I felt like myself.

The next day, before our plane left for home, I decided to come out further, spur-of-the-moment. It was April 1, so I thought it would be fun to come out on Instagram. Since I don't like to surprise people who don't like surprises, especially of this nature, I culled my Instagram followers to only those who I knew were safe people. I then posted a picture of me

---

12 Joshua 1:9 NIV.

at the conference with a caption that read, "Remember those thirty-six years you thought I was a man? April Fools!!! Longest April Fool's joke of my life. Stay pranky my friends."

Apparently, the Dos Equis guy was popular at the time.

I hit post and turned off my phone.

Busting Boxes

When the plane landed, I opened up my phone to what I'll call a torrent of messages in response to coming out on Instagram. Many were congratulating me for coming out and super supportive, but some were not. Apparently, I hadn't removed all my followers who don't like surprises. I had many messages of disapproval for coming out and for coming out on social media with an April Fool's theme. Mind you, no one is owed any special consideration when a person decides to come out, and only the person coming out has a right to decide how they do it. I was now free from my shame and guilt, but apparently not from other people's judgment.

This was my first foray into what I call "box busting." That's when I, as a person, blow up other people's boxes they use to organize life, just by being myself. Box busting happens when someone sees me, at the gas station or the grocery store, and they try to decide, am I a man or a woman—which box should they put me in? When they can't put me into a definitive box, because I look like a woman but sound like a man, or I don't fit a neat standard of man or woman in their mind, their boxes break and they don't know how to treat me or act around me. Now years later, I'm a professional box buster. I walk down the street and people's minds explode.

I'm different now.

I'm memorable.

Before I transitioned, I was perceived to be a run-of-the-mill, cis-white-hetero presenting, introverted male. A dime a dozen.

I could run any number of errands in a specific day: go to the grocery store, drop by the hardware store, stop and get a smoothie, pick up something from a stranger's house off Facebook Marketplace, go back to the hardware store (I inevitably forget something every time), and return home, without raising an eyebrow. Fifteen minutes after someone had an encounter with me, they would forget what I looked like, or that I was even there.

If anyone did interact with me, it went something like this:

I'd say, "We met last Friday when I picked up my smoothie and EVERY FRIDAY before that! You don't remember me? Oh well."

If you think I'm overstating, I can tell you I don't have enough fingers to count the times someone has said to me, "You were at that party/event? I didn't see you there," even though we had talked for ten minutes.

Now I'm different though. Or should I say memorable. I should have anticipated this consequence of transitioning genders, but I didn't.

I thought I'd be able to go about my run-of-the-mill, everyday life without people noticing me, just like I'd done since I was born. When I transitioned, it wasn't motivated at all by the desire to be different. I wanted people to perceive me as a different gender, yes, but I thought, without good reason, people would forget me just like they had in the past.

I thought wrong.

Not only am I now an anomaly in a world that mostly identifies with their sex assigned at birth, but I'm also more myself. I dress differently and am more confident in my interactions. I can be fully seen.

People started coming up to me as if they knew me when in fact they've just *seen* me before but never actually introduced themselves. "I've seen you in here buying groceries before."

Say what?

This phenomenon of being memorable (trans people aren't everywhere in Iowa) and fully seen has also led to some of the more interesting interactions and encounters I've had with strangers over the last few years.

Early on in my transition, Katie and I were at an art museum. I guess I was clearly someone who was transitioning genders because a woman came up to us in the gift shop. The conversation went something like this:

> Woman: "I have to say something to you."
> My inner monologue: *Uh oh.*
> Woman: "I just need to tell you how brave you are. You being you helps so many people."
> Me: "Thank you?"
> Woman (now weeping): "Can I just give you both a hug?"
> Us: "Sure!"
> Woman walks away; me to Katie: "Okay then!"

This was one of the first, if not *the* first, encounter like this. Someone comes up to me, overcome with emotion, telling me how brave I am. Like the woman at the bar who came over to me and my friend Tree and talked with us for fifteen minutes, telling me the whole time how beautiful and brave I was. At the time, I appreciated the sentiment but just wanted to eat my tacos. But the more my appearance changed (multiple years on hormones, longer hair, etc.) the less and less this happened, and the more I realized how special these encounters are.

They are someone giving themselves in vulnerability to a complete stranger, unsure of the reaction they'll get. Their story is bumping into my story in the vast universe, and they want me to know they are a safe space for my story to exist.

Sometimes people aren't willing to put their emotions out there like that, but they'll do things like pay for my lunch. One time I was out to lunch with a friend, and halfway through our meal, a woman came up and laid a twenty-five-dollar gift certificate down on the table, smiled, and just walked away.

"That was weird," I said to my friend.

"That is for you," my friend said to me.

Clearly it was for me and not the run-of-the-mill, white, cis-hetero dude sitting across from me—how people used to see me. I'm different now. I'm memorable now. I'm fully seen.

So seen, that I was once invited to a woman's brunch randomly by a stranger at Target. She asked for my help finding something in the grocery section where I was also shopping. After I helped her find her evaporated milk, she thanked me and kept shopping. Fifteen minutes later, as I was checking out, she got in line behind me and said, "Hi there!" We then had this exchange:

Woman: "Okay, this may sound weird . . ."

My inner monologue: *Uh oh* . . .

Woman: "But I'm having a brunch with a bunch of women tomorrow and wanted to see if you'd be interested in joining us?"

Me: "Oh wow, I truly appreciate it, however I have to fly a kite/go to my kids soccer game/do anything else other than walk into a room full of strange women where I am the awkward trans woman." (Something like that.)

Woman: "Okay."

And that was that. I never saw her again. I've always wondered if she sought me out to help her with her groceries and just became overcome with her own bursting emotions, wanting to affirm a trans woman, to the point of inviting a stranger in Target over to her house. I'll never know I guess, but I was truly grateful for her ability to see me, put herself out there, and affirm me.

Then there are the constant compliments on my physical appearance. They go something like this:

Me, checking out at Walgreens: "Hi!"

Checker (always a woman): "Hi! Oh, I just gotta say . . ."

My inner monologue: *Uh oh* . . .

Checker: "I just LOVE your nails! I love that color/length/shape."
Me: "Thanks!" (Taking my Swedish Fish and leaving.)

It doesn't have to be nails; it could be hair, pants, shirt, sunglasses, anything for that matter.

I'm honestly still thrown when strangers compliment my clothing, which now happens even more because I'm perceived as a woman and not just because I'm transgender. There's a difference between a clerk at Walmart telling me how much she (always a she) likes my physical appearance in order to affirm me, and a woman complimenting my hair because that's what women do for each other.

As I sit here and reflect on all these instances, it is almost always someone with a feminine energy who comes up to me, cries with me, gives me something, invites me to brunch, or compliments my nails or hair in an affirming way. It has rarely been someone who I've perceived as a man.

Even the woman who yelled "Nice shirt!" to me in the airport as I zipped passed on the moving sidewalk was affirming my existence (I was wearing a plain black, cold-shoulder shirt).

I am different now. I'm memorable. I'm fully seen.

Most recently, three of our kids in elementary school submitted essays about why their moms are the greatest. I had *two kids* win the essay contests for their grade! This is what they wrote (unedited with their permission):

Mommo, my second mom, is transgender, which is good to me because she gets to see both sides of the human, men, and women. I know she's the kind of mom that would risk everything to make us live a happy life. To me she is precious! The end. Hi.

I have the best mom in the world. Her name is Nia Chiaramonte. She works in human resources. She taught me to be unique, funny, a great person to be around, and be yourself. She's all those things. I love her so much. She is my hero.

I can tell you, as a run-of-the-mill, cis-white-hetero presenting male, my kids never won any essay contests about me. The staff in the school didn't even know who I was before I came out. But now I'm different, I'm memorable. Something is now unique about me that will never go away. You read those essays, and you can see me. I'm visible now. And I'm so glad I'm visibly me now, because for all the times I wish I could just blend in again, there are now all the awesome strangers that I meet. People who I otherwise wouldn't have encountered in this lifetime if not for being different and someone they will remember. I get to move through the world confidently, in my sometimes wild style, in my own skin, and that draws all sorts of amazing humans in with whom I get to interact.

It wasn't until I revealed my full self to the world that I truly experienced love. Before, I wasn't allowing people to love all of me. But now, I get to experience the love of not only my kids and spouse, friends, and family, but of complete strangers. It's something I could never have fathomed before. When I would bump into another person, bump into their story in the middle of the universe, I used to defer; I would hide my story in favor of theirs. But thanks to the countless people I have encountered over the past few years, I have learned how to bust my own box. I've opened myself up to include my own story as well as other people's. And even though sometimes relationships can be hard, it's a joy to find out more about my story in relationship with others. Giving affirmation to each other, a safe space in the middle of a wild world, is so valuable. And even though most of us think we're not special, we are. And together we're all just a bunch of weirdos.

The Knot

My stomach hurts. Not the *I ate two pieces of pizza and should have thought about stopping but didn't until number four on the way to seven* kind of hurt. No, it hurts because I have an emotional Knot, right in the center of my stomach. I haven't felt it for the last four days.

I'm on my way home from a vacation I've been taking, away from normal life. My wife Katie and I took our newly minted ten-year-old on a trip to the Grand Canyon, a trip planned almost a year prior, which couldn't have come at a better time. I needed a break from that Knot.

My therapist made me thank the Knot in a therapy session before we left, and it made me mad. I hate the Knot. That's where I put all my emotional energy. It goes right there into the center. But she was right. I should be grateful for it. After all, I've lived so many years without my own emotions.

As a peacemaker by nature, I would do everything I could to keep the peace.

Internally . . .

What will they think of me? How should I act? How can I avoid embarrassment?

And externally . . .

Don't say that or they will get mad at you. Don't do that or she will have a poor reaction.

But all these thought exercises have spent mental energy and have come with a bigger cost. After processing all potential emotions in my mind, I never let any of them out, and never even felt them. I lived an emotionless life. Until I came out, I thought I had emotions. I was a person (perceived as a man by most people's accounts), who could cry at a romantic or sad movie. I could get upset and angry at things like wasted leftovers (which my kids should know by now could feed all the starving people throughout the world). I could feel empathy and enter into pain with people. I have had friends who have been hurting deeply, and I have felt it. Turns out, all I was doing was feeling other people's emotions but never having my own.

The first taste of my own emotions was from one of my first therapy sessions. My therapist wanted to try EMDR, the therapy which aims to close the loop on open memories from the past that are hard to put out of your mind, causing you to think about them or causing you to be unable to operate without taking them into consideration in your daily life. This therapy is done through bilateral brain stimulation (BLS), a technique that involves alternating stimulation of the brain's left and right hemispheres. It can be done by following a bouncing light bar with your eyes, sound or music that alternates from left to right, or in my case, by holding a small vibrating buzzer in each hand as they buzz in an alternating pattern.

The first time you experience this therapy, you are supposed to find a calm or safe space that you can go back to in your mind once the hard work of processing old memories begins. Part of the exercise to find that calm and safe space is feeling your body. As I closed my eyes that first time, feeling the buzzing bounce back and forth between each of my clenched hands, the conversation with my therapist went something like this:

Therapist: *What do you feel in your body?*
Me: *I don't know.*

Therapist: *Sit with it, where are you feeling anything?*

Me: *Nowhere.*

Therapist: *Okay, get yourself to a place where you can let go and feel what your body needs to feel.*

Me: *I can't do that.*

Therapist: *Why not?*

Me: *Because . . . if I get to a place where I can let go, I'm not sure what will happen.*

Therapist: *Okay, what do you think will happen?*

Me: *I literally don't know, that is what I am telling you. That is why I am scared to go there.*

It went on like this for about thirty minutes until I got myself to a place where I could let go, and, *pop*, the cork that was bottling it all up for thirty-six years exploded out with such force that it dented the metaphorical ceiling, and in that one therapy session I cried for thirty-six years' worth of life. I'm sure my therapist thought it was nothing, but for me, a dam had burst. Unfortunately, I didn't realize that when you start feeling things, it's not a one-time deal; you feel things all the time and have to do something with those feelings. For me, I had to start stuffing those emotions into my Knot so I didn't get overwhelmed. Now that I was feeling my emotions more than I had in the past, I had to do something with them. If I was having trouble letting them go, the Knot was a tool I used so I could centralize the emotions I couldn't get rid of. I knew where they were so I could go back to them.

That first therapy session was almost a year before this trip with our son, but it seems like an eternity. I picked a bad time to start feeling things. If I would have gone through this therapy ten years ago when my wife had a miscarriage, or even five years ago when we painfully left a church community that we loved while in the middle of adopting a son, I think I could have navigated it without the Knot. But now, in the process of getting real with myself, I needed it.

I needed it not only to deal with my internal emotions (I mean, who wouldn't feel something when realizing the world as they know it was about to start coming down around them?) but to pace myself. I used the Knot as a guide as I moved forward with transitioning. When getting on hormone replacement therapy (HRT), for example, I had to make sure the Knot could handle it before moving further.

There are many ways to transition as a transgender person, and I needed to know what *I* needed to do, not read about someone else's journey and be frustrated because mine wasn't the same. The Knot helped me understand how much I could emotionally handle because the Knot would overflow if I didn't deal with my emotions, making me feel sick. More importantly, the Knot helped when I decided it was time to come out.

Little did I know how much I'd have to utilize that Knot going forward. Stuffing it to the brim at times, hoping it didn't explode.

Now I sit here on a plane, returning from a magical four days with my oldest son and my wife Katie. Traveling the country, taking in the spectacular views (the Grand Canyon is totally worth the trip, by the way), feeling free in my body and free in the world. Flying home, the Knot is returning ever so quickly due to my brain's realization that I have to go back to the rest of life, which includes a lot of pain, a lot of sadness, and a lot of conflict. I hate the Knot, but right now, I can't live without it. So, I say thank you to it, because it lets me know I am alive. It lets me feel my body where I couldn't before.

Most of us trans folks have fairly complex relationships with our bodies. Many of us humans do.

As a young child, I didn't realize I had a body that was different in any way. I grew up climbing trees and playing baseball in the backyard, street hockey on the cul-de-sac, and video games, specifically the Super Nintendo (obviously the best Nintendo), at any friend's house who had a video game console (I got my first console at sixteen years old, the magical Nintendo 64, and played *a lot* of Wave Race).

I was pushed toward typical little boy activities and thoroughly enjoyed most of the things I tried. I played baseball and basketball, and I started to become aware that my body could run, jump, swing a bat, and shoot a ball, where other kids could not necessarily control their bodies in the same way I could control mine. I was comfortable in my skin. Grounded even. Then I hit puberty. It wasn't as though I was naive to the fact that I was in a little boy's body and would soon become a man, it was just that I hoped something else might happen. I hoped I would become a woman.

The disappointment of growing into a man didn't set in right away. It didn't hit me right away when my body started to change because logically, rationally, I knew there was no way around it. Instead, I created a world for myself where I ate a magic mushroom and woke up the next day a woman. Classic transgender fantasy story. You've had one, you've had them all. (Or maybe you have no idea what I'm talking about.)

I thought about having different reproductive parts. I thought about boobs, big ones. Not in the way all my friends were thinking about boobs though. I remember the first and only time I ever saw a *Playboy* magazine in middle school. I was in eighth grade, over at a friend's house for a sleepover when he suggested we go outside. We went up a hill to a garage, and in the space behind the garage someone produced this magazine, to the delight of everyone there. Seeing breasts for the first time was fabulous, and I didn't realize that I *was not* experiencing the same kind of fabulousness that my friends were. All I could think was, *Wow, those boobs . . . would look great on my chest!* It was a weird moment. A bunch of gangly teenage boys ogling over a magazine in silence. My understanding of myself exploding off the pages of a *Playboy* magazine. Suddenly realizing I wished I didn't have facial hair. I wished I was more petite (I was 5'10" in eighth grade). All the things I knew logically couldn't happen.

So, I stuffed the emotions down, like someone who would like to avoid being internally conflicted should do. Keeping them as far away as possible.

I didn't have the Knot yet, so the emotions were just swept under the rug.

No, not under the rug, but under the floorboards.

No, not the floorboards, but in the center of the earth, hoping to never see them again.

But bottling up my emotions, as much as it felt like it served me in the moment, was stunting my growth. When I finally found the Knot, I was able to let go, knowing I had a safe place to put all my excess, seemingly newfound emotions, a place I could put them but not bury them. I hope that someday I don't need the Knot, but today I thank it for allowing me to feel something. Even as I sit here on a plane, that pit of emotion returning, I'm grateful for those who have helped me unlock things deep inside me, and I'm grateful for the Knot, standing by when things get too overwhelming.

Ambiguous Loss

I experienced my first funeral around age eight or nine. I honestly don't remember the year. What I do remember is what I saw, and what I heard. For the first time in my life, I saw sad grown-ups. I heard hushed, low whispers. Words of mourning. I really wasn't sure what to make of it. I was old enough to understand death, but I'd never seen adults exhibit these kinds of emotions before. I'd never seen these sad expressions and droopy body language. A few times in my life I had seen sadness, but it was in adult men downtrodden when their favorite football team took a bad beat. But this, this was different. In my house, these types of emotions didn't exist; I thought they weren't allowed. When my mom got the news my dad had experienced a massive heart attack when I was six, she continued to put on a face of ease, one that tried to convey the feeling that everything would be all right, even though I knew otherwise. I know she was just trying to protect me, and as a parent myself now, I sometimes have to fight the urge to protect my kids in this way too.

It wasn't until I was much older, when my mom nonchalantly told me my dad had experienced another heart attack and had almost died but was fine now, that I realized how deep the denial of my own emotions went. The nonchalance and saying everything is fine. If my own emotions started to show themselves when I was growing up, I likewise vanquished them to a land far away, never to be seen or heard from again. So, when I experienced the death of a friend of the family, I wasn't sure how I was supposed to feel.

Arriving at the funeral, seeing all the people and all their sadness, I didn't understand. I remember milling about, looking up at everyone I encountered, hoping to see someone who wasn't experiencing what everyone seemed to be experiencing, because I didn't understand what was happening. Then I saw the deceased. Lying there. Alone. Gone. I can still remember the intensity of the emotion. It washed over me, filled every crevice of my body, not draining away quickly but filling me to my brim.

What was I supposed to do with this? Looking to the adults in the group for any indication of what I was supposed to do with this aching inside me, this indescribable emptiness, they showed me the way. They shed some tears, then on the drive back home, they talked about other things. In fact, the experience showed me that the pain and grief I felt should be acknowledged briefly, then pushed far away to the far corners of Mordor (if I had known what Tolkien's Dark Land was). Although what I thought I was casting far away, I quickly realized I instead was burying deep within. It wasn't until another family friend passed away unexpectedly a few years later, when I was a bit older, that it hit me. That same feeling, back from wherever it had been flung. I never really dealt with it the first time, never really processed it, and I knew at that moment, attending my second funeral, that it didn't go away. It can't be avoided. Sadness. Loss. Grief.

Although I didn't fully understand all there is to know about loss and grief right then and there, I started to realize these emotions would be constant throughout life. But if I was to learn anything by observing the adults around me, you get rid of that shit as fast as possible. The ignoring—sometimes acknowledging and being angry at, but never allowing in—of the hard emotions seemed to be the extent of it.

Fast forward to today and the sadness, grief, and loss are pervasive. A year after I came out to my parents and family as a transgender woman, my sister is gone—cutting me out of her life for fear that a woman with a transgender experience might have influence on her three kids. I miss her. We used to have fun as kids, her dragging me into rehearsing for plays we were constantly putting on for our parents and neighbors. Even as adults, we loved to argue, Italian style, voices raised but loving at the same time. I miss those conversations.

My parents, while physically still in the same town, are missing from my life as well. This type of ambiguous loss is hard to process.[13] It hurts, understanding they aren't available, emotionally or physically, but still wanting them to be. They are also experiencing ambiguous loss, continuing to talk about me either as if I'm dead, in terms of a son they lost, or like nothing has changed, calling me by my old name as they go.

I feel like I'm losing my faith too. A huge piece of my identity. I held onto it for as long as I could. In fact, when I first came out, my faith was unwavering. I was certain it could stand strong in the face of terrible things said in the name of love. I've learned over the last months that the "love" that drives those things that have been said, the angry and invalidating words, and those things that have been done, the unwillingness to listen or ask questions, isn't the Love that I know. The Love that I still know is the one that sits with you. It takes you as you are. It not only takes you as you are, but it actively affirms you, saying, "You are good and you are right. You are so good, and you are so right."

Losing huge pieces of myself leaves an emptiness. It feels like the death of part of me. The same feelings that I first experienced at a funeral all those years ago.

Many who have gone through the same or similar experiences of loss while coming out have said, "Give it time, they'll come around." And while I truly appreciate the sentiment, and I do have hope that someday these relationships will be restored, I can't hang onto that hope right now.[14] If I do, I'll just keep moving, muttering to myself, "They'll come around, I'm sure of it." Muttering, muttering, until one day I look up, and

---

13 I'd encourage anyone interested in ambiguous loss to read *Ambiguous Loss: Learning to Live with Unresolved Grief* by Pauline Boss (Harvard Press, 2020).

14 If someone comes out to you, don't use the phrase "They'll come around" when talking about a loved one who isn't affirming. You don't know if they will come around or not. Don't say something you don't know. Instead, lead with love. Sit with and be with the person who is revealing themselves to you in vulnerability.

I'm on my deathbed, having missed out on life because I pushed down the emotions of death and loss, waiting for something that never materialized.

This time, though, I have to push into these emotions. Better yet, I have to let them out. I've been holding them steady in the Knot for too long. I've been going and moving for the past year, since coming out, avoiding it all. Today I have to stop. I took the day off work today because I am trying to listen to my body. It's telling me it's time to process, time to move into the grief. I sit here writing in the middle of a local coffee shop, surrounded by groupings of people who I can only envision are part of Christian Bible study groups, mocking me and my lost faith. After all, I've been in those coffee shop Bible study groups.

If your faith was stronger you could get through this.
You clearly never were a true Christian if you are transgender.

But I don't care what people think or what I think they're thinking about me. Today is about me. I need to dig into the grief. I have lost so much.

Even in writing this and allowing myself to feel it, I respond to myself with, "Well, your wife has lost a lot too. Others have lost so much more. This is nothing compared to many people who have it much worse than you."

This kind of thought process is so natural for me, and for many of us. *Count your blessings*, a religious mantra of my childhood still echoes in my mind. And while yes, it's so important to cultivate gratitude in life, this kind of self-talk isn't gratitude. No, this is a mask for the hurt and pain. I don't want to push in, I don't want to process, I don't want to let it out. This fight against myself—the worry about other people's feelings, minimizing my struggle compared to others in the world—is so exhausting. Adding to the very real grief, sadness, and loss.

No, no more. If someone else in my life had gone through the things I am experiencing, I would be sad for them. I would tell them it's shitty.

It's okay to be sad. It's okay to feel it. I can't say that to myself though. I can't let go. I'm sitting in a coffee shop. It feels like there are too many eyes on me. My body won't let me let it out. I have to get out of here.

I've moved to my car and turned on the hot spot on my phone so I can continue writing. I even had to move my car away from the door of the coffee shop. For all my work in therapy, I still can't bawl like a baby in front of fifteen strangers in a coffee shop or even in the busy part of a parking lot. Maybe the adults in my life growing up were crying behind closed doors too. Maybe I should give them some credit, who knows.

Sitting with my grief, alone, in my car, in the middle of a bustling world of people who are shopping, and going about their day, many of whom must also be alone in some kind of grief, I want to let it out so badly. It's starting to hurt my body; this not stopping, not giving into it, always moving forward. With eyes closed, it rushes through my body, from my toes to my fingertips as I write. The sadness and grief, pooled up for so long, draining away through body tremors, tears, and guttural sobbing.

When I open my eyes, although the pressure valve has been released, the residue of this pain, this loss, remains. I thought I could get rid of it by acknowledging it, by speaking to it directly. I guess that's the thing about death, including the death of relationships; even though it becomes more distant each day we get further from it, it always remains. Even so many years after the fact, I'll always remember that first funeral. That feeling. It reminds me that I am alive, and I am human. It reminds me that even in the face of death and loss, Love is all around me. And that Love feels my pain too.

The Woods

Casey came along at just the right time. It wasn't that I didn't have any friends. I had my brother after all, six years younger than me. A constant companion and shadow, especially when it came to backyard baseball games. And there were the other neighborhood kids, although I was four or five years older than all of them. But when Casey came along, also four years my junior, I knew that he felt what I felt, deep in my body. The edge of the woods behind his house were not just a barrier meant to keep us out from the unknown beyond. They weren't just nature's boundary, an easy way for our parents to control us by yelling, "Don't go past the woods!" No, I knew they embodied something else. Exploration. Wonder. Freedom.

I wasn't about to enter the woods alone though. Stories of knife-wielding men lurking, bears ambling (there are no bears in Iowa), and coyotes ready to rip off the arm of a stray eight-year-old did a sufficient job to keep me, a solo adventurer, out. But Casey was the first of my friends to see it for what it was. He saw behind the oaky curtain, and he too was drawn to the miles of woods on the edge of our new housing development, just like I was. I knew the woods were the key. And Casey knew it too.

It was one of those days. I walked outside to a sky so crisp and so blue, the air so fresh, that it could only mean it was still morning, even though the beauty of the day felt complete. As I arrived at Casey's house, he met me with a mood that matched the outdoors. Expectant, excited, full of life and energy.

He had gotten a new remote-controlled car.

If you didn't grow up in the late '80s and early '90s, when it seemed as if RC car (also water gun) technology changed faster than Andre Agassi's hair, the momentousness of this occasion may be lost on you.

Casey had just received the Tyco Ricochet. Retailing for over one hundred dollars, the slogan of this car was, "Drive it like you hate it," because of course it would ricochet off anything.[15] Its characteristic giant rubber tires allowed you to smash it into the wall, bounce it off a tree, throw it down the mountain, and after each thrashing, it would be ready for another race. I remember seeing that car for the first time. Its giant tires gleaming in the morning sun. Just daring us to go crazy with it. Casey, being the generous one that he was and also one to always observe the decorum of age, asked if I wanted to go first.

Obviously!

I gently held the remote control like it was a newborn baby, rolling it over in my hands to get my bearings. We lived in a neighborhood at the end of all new housing developments, which meant there was little to no traffic, so we could play in the street without much interference.

Casey put the car on the ground in his driveway.

In one moment, I hit the gas and we were off, the car flying at what seemed to be seventy miles an hour down the street almost out of our sight.

And then it happened.

You know that thing that happens with a remote control car when you're driving it super fast and super far and it goes out of your remote's range and suddenly you don't have control over it anymore? I immediately could see the consequences of my reckless driving as the glorious Ricochet ricocheted off the street curb at top speed and disappeared into the storm drain.

Time stood still.

---

15 This car amazingly still retails for around one hundred dollars on eBay.

I was mortified.

I had just taken my best friend's most prized possession, that he'd only had for a few hours, and promptly driven it into oblivion, never to be seen again. The crisp, cool air of the summer morning suddenly felt stale. I couldn't breathe. Panic set in.

What have I done? I thought to myself. I sprinted over to the opening in the curb, and true to the advertiser's word, there sat the car, unharmed, albeit six feet below the street, with a taunting steel grate between us and it. I had driven it like I hated it, and it had survived, although out of our reach.

Being the one to drive the car first, the older one, I immediately set about calming Casey down. And true to form, after only about two minutes, he had forgiven me and had resigned the car to its fate.

I, on the other hand, felt terrible.

I quickly devised a plan. We could fish it out of the storm drain.

Yes, yes we could!

I ran to the back of Casey's house, which backed up to the woods, and found a stick long enough to reach the bottom. To this day, I don't understand how I did it, but I hooked the car somehow with a tree branch and pulled it up to the grate. I was elated—for only one second though. Obviously, this amazing car, with these giant wheels, was too big to fit back through the opening on the curb the way it came in. *What?! How is this possible?* I thought. *The laws of physics should be on my side here!*

Never letting Casey see my internal doubt, I suggested we destroy his newly, dearly beloved car again, moments after seemingly rescuing it, by tearing the wheels off. He obliged (what else was he supposed to do?), and I had him hold the car through the grate while I forcefully ripped the wheels off like I was twisting the stem off an apple, praying the whole time for this horrible incident to be over with and everything to be okay.

And just like that, we pulled the car out of the storm drain, popped the wheels back on, and it was as good as new. We were both so elated with what we had accomplished that we forgot the whole part where I had gotten us into the mess in the first place. We both decided that maybe the car (and us) had enough racing for the day, and instead decided to explore the woods.

My house, across the street from Casey's, had a nice, manicured backyard which opened into an area that served as the backyards of at least ten other houses. Nice for playing backyard baseball (until one neighbor built a fence) and capture the flag, but not as exciting as Casey's backyard. Casey's backyard was also nice and manicured, but it wasn't open. Only streams of light could get in through the thick forest that provided a natural boundary and natural shade.

We'd been in the woods behind Casey's house before, but not very far. The woods were the only thing between our housing development and the interstate that curved around our city. It seemed then that there were probably at least five or so miles between us and the interstate, although I remember my parents trying to see if they could hear the interstate sound when they moved into our new house, which should have told me it was more like less than a mile. I didn't care. I knew, just from the little exploring we had done, that you couldn't hear anything once you entered the woods.

Since our sense of adventure and accomplishment was riding high after rescuing Ricochet from the depths, we decided to have a real adventure.

We usually went tromping back in the woods, intent on building a spectacular fort, up in some lightning-struck, mangled tree, but neither of us really had any skills to build anything that resembled a treehouse. So this day, we decided to forgo the usual stopping, setting up "camp," and just walked. The farther we walked, the more we realized we could easily get lost in the woods. In fact, we were completely lost. We didn't care though. We'd either come out on the interstate to the north, hit another street a mile away east or south, or maybe come out at the little league fields a few miles to the west. We were free.

This was the day I realized what it was like to have no expectations.

The woods expect nothing of you, only that you don't get lost. Or do. They don't care. They're just there, waiting, inviting you to come and be. This was my first taste of freedom and the birth of my love for the outdoors.[16]

Since that day, the outdoors have been my safe haven. The place where I can encounter life, God, the universe, and myself. My faith is most easily explained by the mystery of the natural world. I know it's there, providing, guiding, being exactly itself, without expectation of me. I see the connectedness of all things in the woods and the trees. Many of my most pivotal life moments have taken place outdoors. Too many to name. One happened just about four months after I had come out to my family.

I was in a rough spot. It's one thing to understand yourself enough to know you need to get out of the closet; it's another thing to force your way out once people try to shut you back in there.

Things were spinning; I was losing family, friends, and faith. I didn't really know what to do, but I knew where to go to be, without expectation.

Nature.

Since I have a job and a spouse and five kids, I knew I couldn't just drive away and get what I needed. I also had never really traveled alone for an extended period. But after a brief conversation with Katie, I made plans to leave town a few days later for a five-day sojourn. As luck would have it, another dear friend who I had just met was also going through their own journey and agreed to meet me about three days into the trip. I ended up going from the Midwest plains of Iowa, into the Rocky

---

16 It also may have been the birth of what I call "Trippers." Trippers are homemade Moon Shoes that instead of making you bounce, trip you as you go. Casey and I tried to make Moon Shoes out of an old mattress and its springs that we found in the woods, but instead, Trippers were born.

Mountains to a hot spring (meeting a friend from my small high school who is also trans), down to the Phoenix desert, and farther down to the Gulf of California in a matter of eighteen hours. I went from being naked in a mountaintop hot spring to swimming in the chilly February Gulf Coast waters.

Reminiscing recently with my friend about those five days, I told them I didn't remember many of the details of my time during that trip, but I remember how I felt. How it felt to stand naked in the snow on the top of a mountain. How it felt to hike El Elegante Crater in the Sonoran Desert in Mexico. How it felt to swim in the Gulf of California in a one-piece bathing suit for the first time. It all felt like freedom. It felt like I could be me without expectations.

Kudos to my friends, and a stranger who became a friend, for making that kind of space for me on that trip. I'm sure I was a wreck, but I found the freedom I needed in that moment to move forward. The freedom to understand myself without expectations. The freedom to change my pronouns starting then and there.[17] They made space just as the mountains, desert, and gulf did. They allowed me to be without expectation. The only thing I missed on that trip was the woods, the original space maker. The place that first showed me myself long ago with Casey.

The woods showed me what it was like to be without expectations, and Casey made space. That's what good friends do. We make space for one another to be and to know ourselves. We create room for each other to breathe. Casey showed me how to connect to my body. Whether it was exploring the woods, playing street hockey games on the cul-de-sac, building our own go-kart only to send it careening down the street with wheels flying off, or crawling through and exploring blocks upon blocks of suburban storm drains after we had found a secret entrance through an inlet in the woods. I was grounded. Grounded by the freedom to move and the freedom to be. The freedom to feel at home in my body,

---

17 It was just for that trip; I still wasn't out at work or to many others around me.

without any expectations, and that was a gift. A gift that I'd lose and find again along the way. Different friends coming and going from my life who were so valuable, letting me live without expectation. But I wouldn't understand what it meant to truly hold onto life without expectation until I finally busted through the people holding my closet door shut and came all the way out into the light of day.

New Hope

I sat across from an older friend and mentor at lunch yesterday who was asking thought-provoking questions. He asked first if I had any regrets. Did I have any regrets in coming out, and did I have any regrets in the way things happened? The answer to the first question was simple. I came out when I did, at that point in my life, and I have never once said to myself, *What have I done? I've made a huge mistake!*

When relaying this thought to my wife, she reminded me that I'm lucky. She reminded me that other people regret coming out after they do it, surrounded by the devastation of their personal life, wishing they could go back to how it was. I've never felt this. I've certainly felt the sadness of broken relationships as well as the crush of wanting a break from "being out." Wanting to go to the store without people staring at me or go to the movies without having to think about being misgendered, like what had just happened when I sat down to lunch with this friend. Here I was, thinking I looked feminine and cute, and the woman who seated us said, "Welcome, gentlemen." I'd love a moment of reprieve from all that, but never have I regretted being myself for one second.

As for regrets in how things had gone down, I reflected on this question and could only think of a few instances where I would have done things differently. As I processed through this with my friend, I told him about the moments where I would have acted differently, only because what I did in that moment elicited a reaction that was very neg-ative. He asked me if it was mine to own or not, implying that maybe these reactions were other people's emotions, and maybe I shouldn't own someone else's emotions. With more thought, I realized I have owned other people's emotions a lot in the past few years. Because of that, one of the biggest lessons I've learned is to find the boundary between my emotions and other people's. So, the only regrets then are the times that other people's emotions have pulled me out of my own character, where I lashed out in excessive anger, not being true to who I am.

The other question he asked me was, had I thought my parents and family would react like they did? This was a harder question. After thinking about it, I told him I always knew it would be like this, but I never could see it all clearly because I had hope. A hope that I held onto that wouldn't allow me to clearly see what I knew would happen. That's what hope does. It obscures. Whether the chances of something happening are 0 percent, 10 percent, or 50 percent, hope doesn't care. It obscures the facts of the situation, which can be a good thing. Before I came out, I clung to hope that my parents wouldn't abandon me. This allowed me to create a reality where I could move toward freedom and come out. When processing this through with my friend, I realized, if I hadn't had the hope that I would be accepted by my family in the days before coming out, I never would have been able to come out. If I had known I would lose my parents and sister and countless others, I probably would have stayed hidden. But hope obscured reality. It created a possibility of something that wasn't there, allowing me to move forward.

Now that I'm out, beyond the initial event, that hope has returned in a different form. Now, knowing what I know, knowing how my family reacted/reacts/will react to the person that I am, I have a different hope. My current hope obscures what I sometimes realize is the low likelihood that reconciliation will happen. But life isn't always about likelihoods and probabilities, and I have to cling to hope. If it wasn't for that hope, I wouldn't even be here. I'd still be in the closet, living life as a scared individual, or not living at all. Scared to be myself with people, unsure of how to form relationships, unable to step into other people's pain because of fear that it would expose my own. I'd be someone unable to love myself and others fully. But hope prevailed. Because of my initial hope, I'm here. It allowed me to move forward, at the same time obscuring reality and creating a new reality, from which a different hope can spring. A hope that someday, relationships will be restored with my family. As our forty-fourth president said, "Hope in the face of difficulty, hope in the face of uncertainty, the audacity of hope."[18] A hope that someday we'll live in a world where people can be free to love without limits.

---

18 Obama said this while giving the keynote speech in July 2004 at the Democratic National Convention. It can be found in its entirety on YouTube: https://www.youtube.com/watch?v=eWynt87PaJ0.

Privilege

A few years after coming out, I participated in an activity as part of my leadership team at work called Privilege for Sale.[19] This activity was a part of a larger discussion about race and social justice in the world, precipitated by the murder of George Floyd.

The purpose of this activity was to help participants understand their privilege, including hidden corners where we may not even realize we have privileges or where we take our privileges for granted.

For this exercise, all participants are given different amounts of fictional money ($300, $500, $700, $900, or $1,100). They are then given a list of "privileges" they have to buy with their money. They must assume they don't have any of the listed privileges in real life, and each one costs one hundred dollars to buy. There is a list of twenty-seven privileges that participants can choose from, and they are supposed to take their "money" and spend it on the things that would matter most, forcing a choice of certain privileges over others.

For a group of mostly white, mostly heteronormative leaders, it was a great exercise to understand not only privilege in the context of the systems we've created, but also to understand intersectionality. We all have different identities, and some people have multiple identities which are oppressed and discriminated against by the systems that exist, creating unique intersectionality and experiences.

---

19 This activity can be found in the Social Justice Toolbox: http://www.socialjustice-toolbox.com/.

Being made to choose between privileges like "feeling unthreatened and safe in your interactions with authority figures and police officers" and "being accepted by your neighbors, colleagues, and new friends," is not a fun thought experiment, and for me, it became altogether eye-opening when my own privilege was exposed.

I am a white, middle-aged, upper-middle class trans woman and a leader in my organization. Even before this exercise began, I understood that I hold many privileges that others do not. I understood that even doing this exercise, this thought experiment, is a privilege, while not having these privileges is the reality of millions of people living in the US and around the world today.

I realized that based on my race and income level, I hold the privilege of not having to worry about many things that many other trans individuals of color and trans individuals who don't have stable jobs and a good income must think about. For instance, the privilege of "being able to receive medical care, including emergency medical care, without worrying that your identities affect the quality of care that you receive," is something that probably should be on my mind from time to time as a trans woman in America, but it's typically not. I can ignore it because I have good private insurance through my employer. If my insurance doesn't cover me, I can go somewhere else for care. I can pay out of pocket. I can hire a good attorney to advocate for me. I'll be taken more seriously because I'm white. The list could go on and on.

But as I started going through this exercise, my eyes also opened to what I have lost since coming out. As weird as it sounds, this activity broke through my privilege, and it made my heart begin to ache for the things so many have lost or never had, myself included. Those of color, others in the LGBTQIA+ community, and especially those whose identities intersect race, gender, gender identity, sexual orientation, and other systematically marginalized groups, have missed out on the fullness of what this country has to offer simply because of who they are. I had it all before transition. Now, I don't.

In the activity, I ended up with $1,100 to spend. The most out of everyone in the group. I could buy eleven out of twenty-seven privileges. We were given a few minutes to decide what privileges we'd want to buy with our money, then were supposed to discuss with the group. As we went around the room to discuss, people said things like, "This is an impossible task, how am I supposed to pick between these things?" And, "I started wondering if these applied to my spouse and family when I bought them, then I thought I might need even more money for them to have these privileges too. This is so overwhelming." When it came to my turn to share what I had chosen and why, I broke down.

I cried as I explained that I didn't exactly follow directions and pretend I had none of these privileges. Instead, I ended up buying back only privileges I had lost in the last two years. By simply being who I am and coming out, going from a perceived straight, white, upper-middle class dad, to a transgender, lesbian, white, upper-middle class trans mom, I lost a lot. I spent all $1,100 fictional dollars on privileges I had held before transitioning but had since lost. And I wasn't even able to buy up everything I had lost. The list included things like:

The privilege of using public restrooms and restrooms at work without fear of verbal abuse, physical intimidation, or arrest.

The privilege of raising children without worrying about family, friends, and your community rejecting your children because of your identity.

The privilege of receiving validation and acceptance from your religious or spiritual community.

There were so many more. There were other privileges on the list that I didn't lose because my state (Iowa) had protections for transgender people (although the legislature has recently repealed and revoked them), but if I lived in another state, I may have lost them.

Unfortunately, there are a lot of other privileges that don't make it onto lists or state legislatures or are even on many of our minds. Many of them have to do with my entrance into the LGBTQIA+ community, such as no longer being welcome at family events or being able to hold hands in public in certain places, and many privileges are simply things that most cis women have never had their entire lives due to sexism and misogyny. Like the privilege of jogging through a public park without getting catcalled. Before I transitioned, I would have never seen that as a privilege. Now I do. I have a much more visceral understanding of the things my wife has experienced her entire life.

This exercise was so powerful in helping me think through how much privilege I have, and just how much privilege I had as a perceived man who is white and has wealth. I know the past few years haven't felt good for white men, to the point that white men (I'm generalizing here) at times have decided to clap back against a society that they perceive is telling them they don't belong.

But that's not what's being said. The #MeToo movement, the #BlackLivesMatter movement, and a number of other social movements that advocate for people of systematically marginalized identities aren't saying white men don't belong. We're saying this system that was made by white men, for white men, to accommodate white men, has got to change.

It's not that underrepresented and marginalized people are trying to hurt white men by chipping them off the top of the pyramid, but the calls for change are simply pointing out that the culture and social systems that make up the United States of America are not what they should be.

The educational system for instance, is not a system originally built on equity or the ideal that all should be educated. No, the current educational system was built on an idea that only white men should be educated as clergy or to learn a trade. True, we've modified it over time to allow others in, like the Common School Movement in the middle of the nineteenth century, which allowed girls to get an education (although not at the same time as boys), but the base of our current system is over two hundred years old and is built on a foundation and assumptions that most of us now understand to be false and downright harmful. And as far as we've come, inherent inequities in these systems still exist. Title IX for example, a federal civil rights law put in place in 1972 to ensure all students and people in educational settings are treated equally and fairly on the basis of sex, is now being debated in the political square. The law, which makes sure little girls have the same opportunities as little boys, and created protections for women in schools who were passed over for promotions in favor of male colleagues or who have been the subject of harassment, now seems too progressive for some. We're still fighting for equal rights for women, students of color, low-income students, and many others. Many feel like a fish trying to swim down the sidewalk. There aren't always mechanisms built in our societal systems for these underrepresented and marginalized people to succeed, and when there are such mechanisms, they are being debated and torn down.

When I came out, I had a choice to make. Keep hiding and keep all the privilege that came with that, or be myself and lose something. I made the choice which wasn't a choice at all. I had to be me. I had to be free. I lost a lot in the process. But I did gain the privilege of seeing something from a new perspective and that is this: many have been losing out long before me because of their skin color, their bodily abilities, their religion (if it's the wrong one), their gender identity, their sexuality, and a myriad of other inherent identities. I now understand this on a much more intimate level. I see this country and these systems that surround us in a new way. Not made for all to succeed, but as sidewalks that some of us are swimming down. Not only can I see these things, but now I can feel how harmful many of these systems are, and it moves me to change. Our privilege is worth giving up if it means freedom for ourselves and for others. Because as the Black Feminist movement pointed out long ago, none of us are free until all of us are free.[20]

---

20 This quote is often attributed to Jewish American poet Emma Lazarus or American memoirist, poet, and civil rights activist Maya Angelou.

Perceptions

It was a Friday night in Las Vegas, and the vibe was electric on the casino floor. I'd never been to Las Vegas before but was at the ARIA Casino for a human resources conference. I had arrived the day before and was tired, and after meeting a friend for dinner, I headed toward the elevator to get to bed early.

Slot machines whirred and dinged while I meandered across the floor, fascinated by it all. As I entered the elevator, a guy came in suddenly behind me. I hit my button for the forty-second floor, and he hit a button for a different floor above mine.

When we got to my floor, I got out and headed toward my room. I was about ten steps out of the elevator when he stepped out too. I turned the first corner toward my room, heart starting to pick up pace, and seconds later, so did he. I wasn't sure what to do. What if he comes at me? I was lacking any weapon to protect myself. Do I kick him in the crotch? Picking up steam and panic, I rounded the corner to a long hallway with my room at almost the very end. As I power walked toward it, I glanced back. He wasn't there. He didn't come around the final corner. I got to my room, quickly unlocked the door, and rushed inside. My heart rate started to return to normal, but I was unsure of what to do with this experience. It was the first time I had felt any physical unsafety around another person. It was also the second day that I was out publicly, as a woman. I had come out at work, the last area where my identity had been unknown, the day before I left for Las Vegas. I was out and proud.

I was wearing a pink satin tank top with jeans, feeling like I belonged. But suddenly I was having other thoughts.

Is that guy following me?
Is it because of something I did or something I'm wearing?
Is it because he knows I'm trans?

This was new.

It's funny because, being raised as a male in a midwestern suburb, I honestly had not felt physically unsafe other than a handful of times before coming out. Juxtapose this to my wife who felt physically unsafe a lot of the time. Yes, I am 6'1" and she is 5'3", but this shouldn't account for all our differences in felt physical safety. After all, we were together much of the time even as kids, occupying the same space, which should have an objective level of safety if such a thing exists. My wife and I have talked about this a lot. Over the past thirty-five years, I have not had societal norms and constructs telling me to be fearful of everything around every corner, that someone is always out to get me, like she has as a cisgender woman.[21]

I remember in the 1990s when a story was circulating about a woman who was walking to her car at night. She was diligent. She checked for predators behind her, even in the back seat of her locked car. She had her pepper spray and cat-ears keychain out in case she needed to blind and gouge out the eyes of an attacker. Then just as she thought all was clear, a deranged individual reaches out from under the car, cuts her Achilles tendon, and drags her off, never to be seen again. I'm not sure how we could even know how all the above happened in this story, but it didn't matter, it was a story that was circulating that rang true.

As women, my wife and her friends were terrified of this story growing up (clearly that was the purpose), and it turned everyone in the

---

21 Merriam-Webster defines *cisgender* as someone whose internal sense of gender corresponds with the sex the person was identified as having at birth. *Cisgender* is often shortened to *cis*.

world into a potentially dangerous stranger with nefarious intentions. As someone in a boy's body at the time, this story was never directly told to me. When I did hear it, it didn't faze me. I'd just beat this crazy guy up I guess; I don't know. But that's the point, I didn't know what I'd do because I didn't even have to think about it.

As a transgender woman, there are things that physically should scare me. Situations that may not be safe for a woman, but my brain has had to learn how to care. My brain initially didn't know when I should be scared or what might be unsafe. That's how it was informed and built. I used to tell my wife I wasn't scared and never would be, because I was raised as a male and my brain had deep ruts telling me I didn't need to be scared. I thought they'd never change, but I now know that is not true. My illusion of safety and my ability to ignore my mind's fearfulness when there truly isn't anything to be afraid of have slowly eroded away the longer I move through life as a woman. It's an interesting phenomenon.

I used to see safety as a very objective thing. You're either safe or you aren't. But being safe and feeling safe are two separate ideas. Many of us feel safe when, objectively, we might be unsafe. You might have grown up around violence and have no issue with hearing gunshots in your neighborhood at night. You don't feel unsafe, but objectively, you might be. And oftentimes we feel unsafe when in fact, we are objectively safe. Just talk to any Enneagram 6, the fear-based personality who plans it all out, and they'll talk your ear off about all the things that could wreak havoc on their safety, like cracks in sidewalks, faulty folding chairs, and people's elbows inadvertently running into their face and knocking out a tooth (this is a real concern from one of my safety-conscious friends). They feel unsafe all the time, when in fact, objectively they are the most (self) protected people in the world, having created a world of safety for themselves. And all this is to say nothing about the fact that safety is relative, and the level of how safe someone feels in any given situation can vary greatly from person to person. If a child is living in a violent home, they might objectively be safer if they were homeless, living out on the streets, than if they have a roof over their head overseen by abusive adults.

And safety can apply to many things. I can be physically safe but not emotionally safe. When looking at Maslow's hierarchy of needs, I could have my basic needs met, even feel safe at home and in personal relationships, but not feel safe to share my ideas at work for instance.

The issue of safety is a big thing for most trans people if/when they come out. Physical safety, emotional safety, intellectual safety, all of it. When I showed emotional vulnerability when I was coming out, I felt exposed. It was up to the people around me to show me that I was in fact safe.

When I started my coming out process, I started with the people I knew who were the safest. Friends and family who I knew were accepting, loving, kind, and would not cause emotional or physical harm. This was key for me to build up that emotional safety bank, build those relational superstars around me, the scaffolding for when things started to go south. I braided those supports throughout my life: work, home, the kids' school, and other places.

It's interesting how you just know who the safe people are. There were random friends I hadn't seen in a long time that I reached out to because I knew instinctively they were safe people. And every time these people proved me right by creating an environment inside of our relationship where I felt safe; they expanded the space I needed to explore who I was. They did and continue to do this with their words and actions.

Once I got to a point where I needed to come out to everyone, and I started coming out to more people who were emotionally unsafe, one thing was very clear to me: they didn't know they were emotionally unsafe. Because felt safety is in the eye of the beholder—in this case, me. I told a couple of family members that they didn't make me feel safe emotionally, and where I was able to, I told them why. It typically didn't go over well. They thought they were creating a safe environment from their perspective.

The problem is that felt emotional safety has a very hard time existing in the presence of judgmental behavior, which you see when people start talking about religious or cultural or social rules instead of just listening. It's judgment of someone for a life that is perceived as wrong, living a life as a trans woman in my case, and it is judgment of someone's being. That creates an environment where emotional safety cannot exist. Thinking *I know what's best* and having a judgmental attitude toward someone decimates any hope of emotional safety as it demolishes trust.

People I have come out to who have responded well and created safety for me have responded by first listening, then trusting. They trust in who I am and they trust that I know myself better than they know me. They create expanding spaces for us to find ourselves together. People who have hurt me emotionally haven't trusted me and my own story, and in fact have projected their own insecurities about their story onto me, further destroying the possibility of building a safe space where both of us can be ourselves.

The emotional reactions of these people who don't trust me and my own story have something in common. They make my story all about themselves. They see my story as a narrative that is coming up against their story and their narrative in the world. To some extent, that is true. I am presenting a data point for them that doesn't fit with the system they have constructed to order their world. There is a box, a tower, a very large structure of values and beliefs that holds up all of our worlds, and my single data point, me being transgender, seems to throw this whole structure into chaos for some people. The reaction to my news begins by them typically saying how my story can't be. It's wrong. I am wrong.

The immediate recoil against someone else's story that is unlike our own is normal. It's what we do with that initial discomfort that matters. As human beings, when presented with someone else's experience that doesn't fit into anything we've seen before and doesn't fit into what we know to be true and constant, we can ignore it by saying it doesn't exist or we can start to explore it. And that's where the rub starts with those who, for whatever reason, don't trust my story and aren't willing to create space to explore it.

They trust their story, and theirs alone. And this doesn't mean they trust themselves. It means they unwittingly trust the story that's been given to them rather than exploring it fully and making it their own. This is a big distinction, because the people who have reacted emotionally to my story, who really do trust their own story, were able to explore my story and experience alongside their own, even when those two things bumped up against one another. I have built, maintained, explored, and expanded my own story, and when I meet others who have done this as well, we can make room for each other's stories.

And that's really what a relationship is: two stories bumping into each other in the vast expanse of the universe. When stories coexist in harmony and sometimes even gel or merge together, we call it friendship, or maybe even BFFs or soulmates. When the stories can't exist in the same space, we may get mortal enemies (see the stories of Spiderman and Green Goblin, Thor and Loki, or Batman and . . . Superman? Who thought that was a good movie to make?) or we may just not be friends.

Being in relationships means listening to someone's story, not telling them why their story doesn't work, why it doesn't fit with ours. It also means not valuing our story above theirs, creating hierarchy. This is how and why most of the damaging hierarchical structures exist in the world: see slavery. When people have started to do this to me, when they've decided their story is more important than mine and our stories don't fit together, it comes out in the following ways:

- Telling me why God doesn't love me.
- Telling me that I am loved by God but I am sinning greatly.
- Telling me my action is giving God the middle finger.
- Explaining to me that God didn't make me this way.
- Writing a thirty-page paper explaining why I am an abomination.

- Cutting off relationship because maintaining a relationship would be like condoning a pedophile, a drug addict, or something else seen as abhorrent.
- Explaining to me that they are praying for me every day. And not praying that I am happy and healthy (because I am telling people I am happier and healthier than I've ever been), but praying for change.

Do you see a pattern here?

I feel emotionally unsafe because of the church. Damn, that's a hard realization. The place where I should have felt the safest, I felt the most exposed. People telling me they love me—but. They love me—that's why they have to tell me I'm wrong. Friends and family saying, "Just make sure you don't run that Pride flag too high" and "Don't bring your full self to church." They wanted to make sure I "don't cause my brother to stumble" by being me—a typical Bible passage used to control other people's behavior for centuries, when this passage seems to refer to having grace for one another in our differences.[22]

Yes, the church has hurt me badly. Its rules, shame, and message of worthlessness taking me to the brink of death. Thank God there are others who have been through this before who I can join in their suffering. Over time, the church has maligned, defamed, berated, and even killed countless people who didn't fit with church leadership's views of God and the world. "There is one truth about God that we should all aim for," the evangelical Christian church proclaims. However, saying this betrays the fact that there are many truths about God. As many truths about God as there are people in the world.

In the United States, we've seen one part of God for a long time now, and it's a good part. It's the protector, the stoic, steadfast God. But there are other parts. Parts that know what suffering is and can show us

---

22 Paraphrase of Romans 14:13 NIV.

how to enter it as Jesus did. These parts live lives of strength, although their wounds should have killed them long ago (and some have). These lives are resurrected. They are true examples of what Jesus preached and did on the cross. Not fulfilling some sadistic need for blood by God but showing us that there is something better than beating each other down. These lives cling to hope.

And that's the only thing I can hold on to. Hope.[23] I know even when I'm beat down, something better exists. Something worth getting myself up off the floor. Something worth holding my spot in this world, standing firm under the crushing weight of it all. To be true, I am privileged. I am in a place where I can get back up again with the help of a loving wife and kids and the support of friends. Many don't have that luxury.

But as I can, I will continue to find more of myself and share that with others, seeking safe spaces but knowing full well I could get more hurt and wounded along the way. I will do it because I am grateful to folks before me who have shared their stories and want to do the same. But more importantly I will do it for myself. I now know there are indeed times when I'm unsafe. Whether it's in a hotel in Las Vegas or in relationship with someone I care about. And when that happens, I have started to trust myself. I stand up, legs wobbly, and leave when my safety is compromised.

---

23 Seems to be a recurring theme in my life.

The Voice

"I don't want to make this call."

"Well, neither do I."

As my Gen Z coworkers on our procurement team sat across the office from me and argued about who should make the call, I finally stepped in. "I'll do it."

"Oh good, you're a millennial, you like to talk on the phone," they said, relieved they wouldn't have to make the call.

"Yeah, I'm a millennial, but I don't like to talk on the phone. Mostly because I get misgendered on the phone all the time."

"You do not," the three women replied incredulously.

"I do. I'll show you. Give me the number."

I got the phone number and made my way to the phone booth workstation for privacy to make the call to a vendor. We were wondering where a shipment was, and as an HR professional, it was not a call I would normally make, but after two rings, a woman who picked up the other line said hello.

"Hi," I said in the most feminine voice I could muster. "I wanted to call to check on a shipment."

"Yes, sir, let me help you with that," said the voice on the other end.

I let it go. Sometimes customer service folks only use sir or ma'am at the beginning of the call.

"Uh, yes, sir," she continued. "Sir, I can help you with that, sir."

Okay, so it was going to be one of those calls.

"I'm sorry, I'm a woman," I apologized gently for her mistake.

"Oh, I'm sorry, sir," came her reply.

I'm usually pretty good about correcting folks on the phone when they misgender me, being gentle, knowing that they hear a man, and that when corrected, they change their language, but I hadn't encountered this before. I just let it go again.

"Ma'am, let me look into that for you."

Okay, at least she got it right this time.

A few moments later, the representative came back on the line. "Sir, we see it's shipped out to you and should arrive tomorrow. How does that sound, sir?"

"It's ma'am," I said once more, "and that sounds great, thanks."

"Okay, anything else for you, ma'am?"

"No, that's it, thanks," I said, relieved to have the conversation over.

I hung up the phone quickly and exited the quiet booth, where my colleagues were waiting on the status of the shipment, and the details of my conversation. I relayed both, and they stood, mouths agape that I would get misgendered so repeatedly, and again after correcting someone. It wasn't something they had ever thought I would deal with on a regular basis, but I do. My voice is the biggest giveaway that I am a trans woman. When I am in a public restroom, I try not to talk so as not to scare anyone. Over the years of being out, I have become more and more comfortable with my lower voice, but it has taken time.

All my life, I've struggled to find my voice, both figuratively and literally. I was a shy kid who didn't speak up much. As someone who was hiding something, I had a big incentive to stay quiet. And as a kid who was transgender but didn't know it, the one thing I did realize very quickly after my vocal pitch deepened was that I didn't like the sound of my own voice. It gave me dysphoria. I knew as a kid that my voice wasn't going to stay high like most of the girls and women I knew, but when it happened, it was disappointing. To cope, I turned to accents and voices. I was always using weird voices and accents to cover up my real voice, so by the time I figured out what was causing my discomfort thirty-five years into my life, I was speaking in ridiculous characters and accents approximately 40 percent of the time.

I can only do obscure accents like Dr. Doofenshmirtz from *Phineas and Ferb*, Shaquille O'Neal, Edna Mode from *The Incredibles*, and the occasional Muppet or other made-for-my-kids' stories character accents, but I digress.

When I first came out, the relief of being myself fully around other people was overwhelming. I didn't care what I sounded like because I could finally relax. Over time though, the sound of my voice started to produce more and more dysphoria.

I eventually decided to go to a speech therapist who specialized in helping trans women.

She was a lovely woman, a voice coach originally who had one trans client, and then once the word got out, all the trans ladies started going to her. By the time I saw her, she was firmly entrenched on the "people who are trans friendly" list, and I was excited to see what she could do.

We worked over the course of a few months to increase my vocal range through a myriad of exercises common for folks in the singing profession. I'd carry a straw with me, and when I was in the car would hum up and down the scale through the straw, pushing my range further and further.

She also helped trans ladies with comportment. For some, transitioning to the opposite gender can be extremely difficult. Especially when someone might have been conditioned to be hypermasculine to cover up their femininity. She worked with me on how to stand and walk, also making sure I didn't manspread my legs anymore when sitting down in a chair.

I appreciated the time and energy she put into working with me, but in the end, it felt like I was putting on another costume. Trying to approximate how society thinks a woman should act felt fake to me. How far did this really need to go?

I did countless exercises, all helping me do the same thing I could do since I was young: throw my voice toward any number of characters in a higher register. It felt much like it did during that first experience at the drag restaurant Hamburger Mary's. Each time I tried out a new voice, it felt like I was putting something over the top of myself, rather than expressing myself.

I realized a few months into therapy that there is a difference between gender dysphoria, the thing that causes me discomfort because my brain and body are not in alignment, and the discomfort we feel in society when we're not meeting the expectations of others. For me, I've had to think about this with my voice. Was I wanting to change it because I truly cringe with dysphoria when I hear myself? Or do I cringe because others have told me my voice isn't high enough to be a woman and I won't be a proper woman with a low voice? Is the judgment from others the thing that is driving my dissatisfaction with myself? We all do this to some extent. We're not tall enough or skinny enough or have clear enough skin or whatever we think we're supposed to have because of the expectations of society. As I think about this distinction, I've come to realize that I do like my voice. I only rarely experience true dysphoria because of it, and more often feel judged by others because of it. When someone misgenders me, I used to think, *If only my voice was higher, then they would see me as a woman.*

But now, I understand that thought is just me changing to meet other people's needs. I'm trying to meet their expectations of a true woman. I call this *as-long-as inclusivity.* Many people don't have a problem with trans people, especially trans men, as long as we meet the expectation for a binary man or woman. We just need to make sure we have a high enough or low enough voice, we blend in, we don't make people feel uncomfortable. As long as we can do that, we're included.[24]

---

24 "As-long-as" inclusivity is a rising trend in the United States. People don't want to be outright hateful, but they also don't want to feel uncomfortable, leading to standards applied to people who are different. You can be an immigrant as long as you assimilate. You can be trans as long as you're not making people uncomfortable.

But what about those of us who are tall, broad-shouldered women with deeper voices?

I have to analyze my own discomfort on a daily basis. Is it about me and my discomfort with myself? Or is it about others' perceived discomfort with me? Once I realize that I'm doing something for other people's benefit, I can stop. I can focus on myself and what truly brings me dysphoria, and what brings me happiness.

In the end, other people's opinion of me is none of my business, but my opinion of me is what matters. Only time will tell where I land with my voice, and if it turns out to be dysphoria-inducing down the road, I will do something about it. But for now, I can't imagine a time where I can't sneak up on my kids and in my best Shaquille O'Neal impression say, "Hey, kids, when you're tall like me, you ball like me," and watch them roll their eyes, wholly unimpressed. It overcomes any dysphoria I have every time.

Finding Nia

Nia,

Well, here we are. I want to tell you I'm writing this letter from the other side, but the trouble with that is that there aren't two sides to this thing. It's circular and it's nebulous. It ebbs and flows. But nonetheless, here we are. Strong, resilient. Still standing. Still joyful. Still loving. Your body is beautiful. Your heart is still invested. You haven't changed course, although your love has taken you to places you've never imagined. The feelings you've experienced along the way are very real and not imagined. You've transcended them, incorporated them into your story, into your body, opening yourself to hurt and pain, and joy and love. You haven't side-stepped the hard stuff but have moved into it even when it seemed impossible. To where we are now, a place of self-knowing and a place where judgment has no home. This is the place where you know yourself to such a level that you can let others in and show them who they are in the process. A real symbiosis of love alive in the world. Keep going. Forward, backward, sideways, and slantways. Just keep going. You will never reach the end, although the end is right where we are. Always.

With Love,
Nia

I wrote this letter to myself from my future self, in a moment of clarity in the first year of my transition. I understood at that moment that this kind of journey isn't a straight line. It winds its way through the forest of euphoria and the desert of dysphoria on a moment-by-moment basis.

Even so, as I sit reading that letter years after I wrote it, I see something I didn't see before.

The letter from the future implied that I would keep moving, going in one direction or another. I never could have fathomed that there may be a point in my life where time stopped altogether, where movement was halted. But then it happened in 2020. Thanks, COVID-19.

It started one day when I was feeling melancholy. Many of us had those feelings in quarantine; however, I couldn't readily identify the source of this one. Was it the fact that I couldn't hug my friends anymore? Was it that I couldn't go into work for months on end? Was it that it was raining cats and dogs that day and it felt like the sun had burned out forever? It was all those things, but it was none of those things.

As I dug down to feel my feelings (Geesh, how often do I have to do this?), I realized it was grief. I know I wasn't the only one feeling the grief. It could have been caused by any number of things in the pandemic. Normalcy, routine, or comfy office chairs lost. (Seriously, the chair we had at home for our makeshift home office sent me to eleven physical therapy sessions, a cortisone shot, and surgery for my shoulder.) It wasn't any of those things though. As I reflected further, I realized what it was: momentum lost.

Again, I know I'm not the only one to feel those things during that uncertain time. Momentum of projects derailed. Momentum of work-out routines hijacked. Momentum of wedding planning stuck in limbo. Momentum halted all over the globe. My momentum, though, seemed very specific to me and other transgender people actively in transition. Momentum of gender transition halted. I realized that up until that moment, while I wasn't necessarily looking way down the road to the "end" of the transition process, I was looking at the next step. One foot in front of the other. Step by step. Day by day (remember that TGIF show *Step by Step*? Suzanne Somers was amazing).

I always had some new activity, small victory, or milestone that was next, even if it was months in between them. Another electrolysis appointment. Another laser hair removal session. A surgery consulta-tion. Suddenly, in March 2020, all those things stopped. Most trans sur-geries were considered elective and nonessential and not allowed in most states. Hair removal was considered a cosmetic procedure, and cosmetic procedures were halted all throughout the United States. No electrolysis or laser hair removal.

It suddenly felt like time, all time, was being *wasted*. I wasn't doing the productive things that I could and should be doing to move myself forward. So, like many others, I had to stop. Evaluate what really mat-tered. Learn new hobbies to fill my time like playing the piano and mak-ing my own kombucha.

And in the end, like many others, I gained perspective, particularly when it came to my transition. The point of transitioning is to align my brain and body and to help others in the world perceive me as I perceive myself, as a woman. But without relationships, external transition means so much less. I had to step back again and evaluate, what am I doing for myself to ease my dysphoria, and what am I doing to please others or to avoid others' judgment?

And with all the uncertainty in the world during that moment, one thing I was sure of: if I didn't know who I was and what I wanted, I was going to be at risk of losing myself to the judgments of the loudest voices.

"You're going to hell for all of eternity."

"You are leading so many people astray with your lifestyle."

"I'm not even going to tell you how much this hurts me."

"You are a terrible human being."

"We can't be friends anymore."

"I wish it was how it used to be."

"You used to be so handsome."

"Why are you taking (Deadname) away from us?"

"You're an insult to the family."

"I won't be moving forward with Nia."

These statements by friends and family and church leaders had started to bury me. That confident me who came out, having already dug through the shame and worthlessness, knowing who I was, started to be muted by hurtful statements. Before COVID though, I would keep moving forward, letting the junk roll off me. But now, at a standstill, it started to be overwhelming.

There were so many affirming voices too. In fact, many more affirming voices than those who were judgmental. But it didn't matter. Hurtful words ring longer.

Even now, I think all these people, including my family, truly believe they still love me. Or at least they love the person they thought I was on the outside. But it never did and still doesn't feel like love to me.

And during a global pandemic, where thoughts rattled around like a ping-pong ball inside a steel drum, the hurtful thoughts won out. I found myself feeling lost and alone.

Fortunately, just by putting pen to paper, I realized I hadn't lost myself. Others have just tried to bury me, repeatedly. But the thing about finding your Knowing is that you never really forget it. You know the feeling of freedom that comes with telling people who you are. Your Knowing is so strong, and even if buried in other people's shit, it gives off a resonance so only you can find your way back to it.

In fact, I have realized that I found Nia a long time ago. I have known her since I was young. I just kept trying to put her somewhere safe from people dumping their shit on her, always able to come back to her, over and over, but never letting her into the light for fear that she would get hurt. When I finally had the courage to dig her all the way out and realize that she and I are the same, I was free. I now realize that I will never lose her again. People may try to bury me with their own emotional garbage or their narrow view of God, but they can't. I will always know where I am.

Rude but Affirming

We stood in the backyard of our five-acre country property, overlooking the rolling hills of Iowa. I asked the contractor what it would take to upgrade our older, large propane tank to something smaller and more unobtrusive.

He looked at our garage, down at his clipboard, over to the house, then back to the garage and said, "Well, does your husband need heat out in that outbuilding? If he works out there a lot, it might be something to consider."

Stunned at his assumption that I was married to a man, while at the same time suddenly flattered that he saw me as a woman, most likely a cis woman, I didn't know what to say so I just mumbled, "Uh, no, we're fine."

"You may want to check with him first," the contractor added, again making me feel good about being perceived as a cis woman, but this time I couldn't ignore the rudeness of his assumption that I, a woman, needed a man to make this decision for me. "I don't think my wife needs heat out in the garage and neither do I."

Now he didn't know what to say. "Uh, okay," was all he could muster, realizing his mistake.

I didn't utilize his services.

But this encounter did get me thinking.

One of the fascinating things about gender transition is that because of my differences, I now have a unique experience in my view of how we as society categorize people based on their perceived gender and then behave in certain ways toward them based on that categorization.

I have my experience of what it was like to move through the world as a white man, all the privilege, control, and power that came with that, and now what it's like to move through the world as a woman. What I'm about to say is nothing new for cisgender women, but for someone who is just starting to experience these societal expectations and behaviors, it's jolting. I'd like to tell you about some of the more interesting interactions I've experienced where people have perceived me as a woman and how it compared with my experiences when I was perceived as a man.

To begin, I must say that while I can assume the motives of the people I'm interacting with and will tell you here what I think those motives are, I may be way off. We can never understand motivations based only on behavior. So, while I might think I know why someone refuses to talk to me while they're scanning my items at the grocery store, I can't know for sure. Maybe they don't actually hate all trans people like I'm assuming. Maybe they're just tired. Maybe antisocial in general. Or maybe they can't speak. Whatever their motivation, I can relay how the situation made me feel.

One of the most interesting interactions happened right after I came out. I experienced what I will call "categorization paralyzation," which occurs when someone can't quite put you into a category, so they just pick the one they think fits best and jam you in so they can maintain the status quo for their categorizations.

I had a friend who I was just getting to know, and we were getting along great. We were going out for coffee often, and when we talked, we really connected. Then I came out. He was very happy for me and was wonderful about it. I texted him a few weeks after that and asked if he wanted to get breakfast. He didn't text me back for a long time, and then when he did, he said he was busy.

This happened about three or four more times. I would text; he would wait to text back but then say he was busy. Finally, after this had gone on for almost three months, I decided he must be too turned off by me coming out as transgender. Realizing this wasn't a fair assumption to make, I decided to do the reasonable thing and just ask.

His response wasn't something I expected. He texted a week later and said it wasn't my transition, but the fact that he adhered to what is known as the Billy Graham rule.[25] His own personal ethic wouldn't let him be with me, a woman, alone.

This was one of the first times I had the pleasure of being gendered correctly, and it was an amazing feeling to be seen for who I am, a woman. But this categorization paralyzation destroyed a beautiful friendship. He couldn't understand where to put me, so he put me in the place he thought was the most honoring, which was to treat me like he'd treat any woman. In his life, he doesn't spend time with women by himself. (I have no judgment of him for this ethos as I don't know why he holds it; however, I do think that this Christian-based rule leads to the systematic oppression of women.) This was also the first time that I experienced what I call "Rude but Affirming" behaviors from people.

Rude but Affirming behaviors are typically behaviors displayed by people (mostly men) who end up putting me into the "woman" category in their mind and treat me how they would other women, which ends up being sexist and demeaning at best. He treated me like a woman, which was affirming, but in following his rule, he treated me misogynistically, which was rude. As a trans woman, these behaviors may affirm my entry into womanhood, but they are rude in general.

I want to say again that these examples I've experienced are only affirming because of my transition. Cisgender women go through these things on a daily basis and have their whole lives, and they aren't affirming, they're just rude (or worse) and are behaviors born out of a patriarchal society.

---

25 The Billy Graham Rule, also now called the Mike Pence Rule, is a misogynistic set of practices outlined in the Modesto Manifesto from 1948. The Manifesto aimed to "avoid any situation that would have even the appearance of compromise or suspicion," leading to church-sanctioned sexism for the last seventy-plus years.

As I started to get further along in my transition, Rude but Affirming continued to rear its ugly head. As my hair got longer, and my body was becoming more feminine, it was harder for people to clock me from afar.[26] One day, as I was walking through a park, a man inside a truck that had tires far too large for its own good, catcalled me. Not in the regular way, but in the *I want to have sex with you right now* kind of way. Something that never had happened to me when I was perceived as a man. Rude (and then some), but Affirming.

Then there were people who started to come in for a hug without asking, because when they greet people, there's a male greeting (handshake) and a female greeting (hug). And don't get me wrong, I love hugs, and if those are your categories for greeting people (maybe reflect on the need for it first), by all means, you do you. You just need my permission, at least once, to make sure I'm okay with your hugging. When I was perceived as a man, this personal bubble was rarely encroached on as I was in the "handshake" category.

There are also now men who encroach on my personal space to explain something to me because they think that getting closer apparently helps them get their point across. This personal bubble encroachment *never* happened to me before I transitioned, with the expectation of someone purposefully trying to be aggressive. It happens much more often now when (it seems) intentional aggression isn't the motivation. Again, this is a behavior that cis women have lived with their whole lives and is terrible. But for a trans woman, Rude but Affirming.

Of course there are the times I've been asked to "check with my husband" or "check with my spouse" before making a decision when a maintenance person is in my home trying to fix something. I was recently

---

26 *Clocking* is when someone realizes I am transgender without my disclosure. For more on clocking, and why it can lead to unsafe situations for trans people, and to understand our current president's endorsement of it, check out "Clocking for Beginners" by Marilyn Drew Necci (July 22, 2020) at https://rvamag.com/queer-rva/clocking-for-beginners.html.

getting a quote for new windows, and the technician asked me if "everyone who was in a position to make a decision would be present." He quickly backpedaled understanding how sexist this sounded. Rude but Affirming. I don't know how cis women who have had this happen resist the urge to punch these men in the face.

I've had the door held open for me, only to be slammed in my face. The man who opened the door first saw me from afar and perceived me as a woman. As I got closer, he perceived me as a man and decided that the common courtesy of holding a door open for someone should be based solely on that person's gender, and slammed it shut forcefully before I could go through. This was not a Rude but Affirming behavior but gets at the same categorization paralyzation.

I could list more examples of these behaviors which include weaponization of a woman's body; putting the onus on women to explain themselves or their behavior; men trying to push their own fear of women onto women; and a multitude of other run-of-the-mill sexist, misogynistic, and potentially violent behaviors.

I would have never experienced most of these behaviors from other people if I hadn't transitioned and if people's view of me and expectations for me had remained male. But I transitioned, so people now can see me how I have always seen myself. And now many in society have placed new expectations on me as they categorize me as a woman.

It's sad that as a trans woman, I sometimes reach for validation and affirmation from these terrible behaviors. It's sad that a whole gender of people is categorized in a certain way, put in a box and told how to behave. That's not to say that men don't have a box too. The difference, it seems, is that white men created the boxes and from personal experience, theirs is full of power, control, and dominion (a generalization, of course).

There is no way I could have ever gotten to this point if I hadn't transitioned. Before, as a kind and considerate man, I understood the plight of women in society. I didn't participate in terrible behavior toward women (or at least I don't think I did), and even though I knew it wasn't true, I hoped no one else did either. But I didn't understand how a patriarchal society affected women until I lost much of the privilege that was based on my gender. Nigerian novelist Chimamanda Ngozi Adichie once said gender as a function of society today is a grave injustice.[27] I now understand a little bit about what she means.

It's unfortunate that it took me transitioning to begin understanding the second-class way women are treated in society. It's also unfortunate that this treatment is something that confirms my womanhood. This is my daily struggle. I don't want to get my affirmation from a society that tells me I must meet this new set of expectations and that I must stay in a new box to be affirmed as a woman.

One of the saddest parts of all this is that there are trans-exclusionary feminists, women (like the outspoken J. K. Rowling) who would argue that it's precisely because I haven't had to deal with this terrible behavior my whole life that I'm not a real woman. Unfortunately, that argument leads to womanhood being based entirely off the bad behaviors of men.

I hope to one day get to a point where many of my cisgender sisters are and have always been able to see and call out these behaviors for what they are: not just rude, but demeaning, harmful, offensive, violent, and definitely not affirming of womanhood. We are women because we identify as women and that's enough. Let's stop categorizing each other all together and allow each other's stories and identities to simply be.

---

27 Chimamanda Ngozi Adichie said this during a TEDx talk in 2011 titled "We Should All Be Feminists."

Certainty

I miss certainty.

I was up last night in the middle of the night for an hour. Just thinking about it. Its absence haunting me, jeering at me, daring me to keep living. I didn't realize I missed it, even though I haven't had it for a few years. Honestly, I started losing it when I had kids. No, I'm not talking about my hair. I'm talking about one of those things that you don't know what you've got 'til it's gone. And when it's gone, it's gone.

When I first came out to my dad, he asked Katie and I to meet him at a coffee shop. At one point during the conversation, I pleaded with him to give up his certainty. It was getting in the way of us having a relationship. He was certain I was sinning. He was certain that who I am is wrong. He was certain that all the strife in his life was my fault. He was certain God still loved me. He was certain he still loved me, even though we don't talk anymore. He was very, very certain about his place in the world. Theological certainty. When I asked him to give up some of his certainty, he responded, "I like my certainty. I don't want to let go of it, and I'm not going to."

It was crushing to hear those words at the time. It's crushing right now writing them out. When someone is unwilling to let go of their "knowledge" about the world, it's hard to find growth, relationally or otherwise. I know this from experience. I used to be certain too.

If I'm being honest, my certainty started to erode very early in life. I'd go to church, Wednesday nights and twice on Sundays. I'd go to Christian school every day where we'd learn about God. I'd hear the lessons preached: A God who loves me. A God who also needs me to burn in hell because I'm a sinner. A God who cannot reconcile these things without more bloodshed, specifically his own son's. It was hard for a logical kid like me (and maybe any logical kid) to ever bite down on all of it. It wasn't something that provided a lot of certainty deep down in the first place. It did, however, provide a sense of certainty in the everyday.

Uncertain of what the day held? Pray. Uncertain if my parents' friend's cancer would go away? Pray. Uncertain of what to do in a specific situation? Ask God. Check the Bible for answers. Every answer is in there after all, you just have to look. Afraid of the dark? Know that God loves me. Afraid of being kidnapped? Know that God has plans for me. Afraid of doing poorly on a math test? Pray like hell. It will all work out for my good. After all, I do love God.

This may sound like a sarcastic critique of my faith and the certainty that came with it, but I want to be clear, that faith did get me through thirty-plus years of my life. It was helpful for forming who I am. In the long run though, it also took away my own responsibility, emotion, feeling, and real critical thought of any given situation or relationship.

My certainty started to unravel in earnest when our first pregnancy ended in miscarriage. All I wanted was to be a parent. All the church ever told me to do was be a parent and raise good, godly children. I was doing everything right. I was obeying all God's commands. Then we lost our first child at thirteen weeks. I thought it was a mistake. Like many first-time potential parents in shock, we asked them to check again to be sure. But this time they were certain, and suddenly I wasn't. I had so many questions. First and foremost, why? Why did this happen? How could a good God allow it? My certainty started to erode further when fellow Christians said things to us like, "This was God's plan" and "God knows what he's doing" and even "You must have done something wrong for this to happen." It provoked more questions from me that were answered with, "We don't know why God does what he does," which, while maybe theologically accurate in the evangelical Christian system of belief, isn't kind or helpful when said to someone who is grieving. And this was the tip of the iceberg. Asking the question "How does a loving God cause this?" leads to questions like "Is God loving?" If God is loving, why does he send us to hell for our uncleanliness? And just like that, the facade of certainty that was my daily life cracked wide open, daring me to fall in.

I was good though. I saw the cracks and evaded them. I learned how to live with the questions. I studied Christian apologetics, which tries to provide a rational basis to fill the gaps, and started to rely more on prayer. But you know those animated cartoons where someone is in a rowboat and water springs through a hole? They stick their finger in and another hole sprouts, water streaming in, until the person has all ten fingers and toes and even nose plugging holes in the boat? It was like that. When we're laughing at the person in the rowboat as their boat goes down, we tend to forget about how they're now without a boat. And depending on whether they can swim and how far they are from shore, they may die. Not so funny anymore, eh, Looney Tunes?

Eventually my cracks caused massive holes that couldn't be repaired, and I found myself without a boat. I started to question everything. No one had good answers. "Have more faith." "Pray more." "You're sinning to even ask these questions." "The devil wants you to question, so don't." Not answers so much, but certainty to patch a boat that was at the bottom of the lake. I found one thing and clung tight. Love. Love seemed to hold up over time. I could be certain that Love conquered all.

Then I came out as transgender. A moment in time where I took control of my own story like I never had before. I was certain again. Certain that I knew nothing except who I was, and I needed to start there. At that point, I was pretty sure things couldn't get more uncertain, but I was wrong. When you come out as trans, your world is turned upside down. Any confidence you might have in moving through the world is altered. It's anything but certain.

I wish I could say there was a moment where it clicked. And while there were many things that helped me in a positive way on my journey, particularly some books I read about certainty and love, it was a slow burn.[28] I went to therapy; I allowed myself to question and allowed myself to answer. I realized that I was the one. I was the one to send a meal to a friend who had cancer. I was the one to dispel my fears by moving toward them. I was the one who could study for the math test. I was the one responsible for my life.

Taking control of our own lives, instead of codependently giving all our emotions, fears, hopes, and dreams to God, takes work. It's taken years to undo the pathways in my brain that defaulted to saying, "God's got it under control," while walking away from a situation.

Now, I first ask myself, is the thing I'm worrying about or the situation I'm in even mine to handle? If so, I do it or I don't. Or I do something in between. If I'm scared and I can't cope alone, I find a friend who I can touch and who can hug me. There is no longer an esoteric God, I Am, outside of all things. There is only I Am in us. God in each one of us. And while my life feels good to live now, there are moments I crave that easy certainty that only came with saying a prayer. *God, please don't let me die young and leave my kids and spouse. Please help my friend not to die. Please let me have a successful surgery. Please, please, please.*

Now, without my certainty, I sit in my moment of fear. I let it do its work. I examine it and I work through my fear. Because that's really what it comes down to—I'm scared. It takes much longer than a quick prayer, but in the end, I have a boat that won't sink. A boat that, while it can sprout leaks, I know I can bring it to shore and get it patched. I now live a life where I am in control of everything, and I am in control of nothing. Both/and. And I am certain of only one thing. True Love is beautiful.

---

28 Peter Enns, *The Sin of Certainty* (HarperOne, 2016); Jacqueline A. Bussie, *Love Without Limits* (Broadleaf Books, 2018); Wm. Paul Young, *Lies We Believe About God* (Atria Books, 2017).

Love of self and Love of others. The rest I'm uncertain about, but I sit with an open posture toward the universe.

One day I hope to have another discussion with my dad. One where he says he's uncertain, or at least less certain than he used to be. Or at least some sort of conversation at all, because that will mean something has changed. And in the end, that's all I can hope for, uncertain in the waiting.

The Name Game

Hi, my name is Nia. Although you knew that already. Nia wasn't always my name, though you probably guessed that by now too. Picking out a new name is a big deal for a transgender person. It's a moment in time we get to control what happens next, and most of us don't take it lightly.

For me, it was a struggle. When I was assigned male at birth (AMAB),[29] the first perceived male grandchild in the family lineage on both my mom and dad's sides of the family, it was a big deal. There was a tradition on my dad's side of the family where the first son would get the father's name as his middle name. My dad's middle name is the same as my grandfather's; my dad then named me after my grandfather, and I would give my first son that same name as his middle name. That was how the tradition was supposed to continue. But there was one tiny problem; I'm a woman and the name didn't fit.

So, when it came time to choose a new name, I really struggled. The moment didn't present itself to me like a single moment in time, but rather a series of moments, leading to a name change.

First, there was the persona. Many trans and nonbinary people need to try on different names, pronouns, and expressions before really understanding who they are. For me it was no different.

I decided to create a social media profile, one that wasn't connected to my "male life" at the time, to hopefully be able to explore more freely without consequences should I decide this wasn't what I needed. The

---

29 For more info on this and other LGBTQ+ terms and acronyms, visit the Trans Language Primer at https://translanguageprimer.com/.

problem, of course, is that the first step in creating any social media profile is recording your name for all the world to see.

I remember the first time I created a profile. For some reason, I hadn't considered what my name online would be and that it would need to be different. I paused, immediately shut down the process of account creation, and spent the next five hours looking at names and name meanings. After deep dives into countless name/origin of names websites, I settled on the name Eva Caruso. A pseudonym I chose because Eva means "mother" or "giver of life" and Caruso means "close-cropped hair," or more generally "boy or lad." I felt stuck in between man and woman, so I chose a name that represented both.

For months, I was Eva, she/her pronouns, someone who took a lot of selfies, but then something happened. I went to therapy and realized that this wasn't it. Eva, my persona, wasn't my whole self. She was a step in the right direction and what I needed at the time, but she wasn't complete. Having to put something over the top of myself to feel whole wasn't going to work in the long run, but it is really hard to find yourself when you don't know who you're looking for. So, when I realized I was transgender, I had to evaluate. Was I going to use she/her pronouns, maybe they/them? It took some soul-searching, many months, and over 3,500 miles of travel in the span of five days, to discover that, yes, I am a transgender woman. Once I knew who I was, I had to figure out what people could call me.

For me, choosing a name meant including my past, but I want to make a disclaimer here. Many trans and nonbinary individuals want nothing to do with their past. When they change their name, they want to leave their old life behind, and that is completely valid. Just as it was valid for me to include who I was and still am into my narrative going forward.

I felt like I had lived a relatively authentic life, as much as I could have up to that point being a closeted trans woman, and I wanted to include that story going forward. For me that meant choosing a name that was derivative of that family name that was passed down to me. I wanted to honor my grandfather, my father, and my son. So I chose Nia.

In doing my research, I found out that my grandpa, who I was named after, also changed his name when he came to the United States from Italy. I never got a chance to meet him, but now, in changing my name to Nia, I have more in common with him than I ever did when we shared a name.

I had chosen a name but I still wasn't settled. There are *so many* names to choose from in the world. How would I know I had chosen the right one? Couldn't God just give me a new name? Seems like that happened a lot in the Bible. Or at least maybe I could get a sign that I'd chosen correctly.

Then we went to that fateful conference in New Mexico. There, at Katie's behest, we waited in line to meet one of the conference speakers, Rev. Dr. Jacqui Lewis, senior minister at Middle Collegiate Church in New York City. When we spoke to her, my wife told her how much we had wanted to meet her and introduced me for the first time by my name: Nia. Dr. Lewis immediately said, "Oh, I love the name, 'purpose'!" I said, "What's that?" She said, "Nia means 'purpose' in Swahili." I almost broke down weeping right there. Before that moment, I was unsure, scared, and doubting my path and my new name. After that moment, I was sure. My name is Nia.

But it wasn't that easy.

As a trans person, once you are confident in your own name, it feels like you can take on the world. You go and tell people what your new name is (if you're out), and you hope that people will respect it. The first time someone who knows your new name calls you by your old name, which is called *deadnaming*, it feels like a punch in the gut.

In case you are unfamiliar with the term *deadnaming* or need a refresher, Wikipedia is here to help:

"Deadnaming is the act of referring to a transgender or nonbinary person by a name they used prior to transitioning, such as their birth name. Deadnaming may be unintentional, or a deliberate attempt to deny, mock, or invalidate a person's gender identity."[30]

There are many reasons people deadname transgender and nonbinary people. The most common reason is that they may be adjusting to a new name after knowing someone by another name for years. But they may also be doing it on purpose to show they reject the person's new name and identity. These two are the most common reasons for deadnaming someone.

It also is typically easy for a trans person to distinguish between an intentional deadnaming and an unintentional deadnaming.

For me, although I was confident in my new name, I wasn't all the way out yet. I changed my social media profiles from Eva to Nia and I knew that was my name, but I lived with my deadname each day.

When I finally did get to tell other people my new name, I was so happy. Then the deadnaming started in earnest.

Most people got it right away. They switched from my deadname to Nia and never looked back. But some didn't get it. It was harder for them. Whether it's the years of history between people or the fact that when people are stressed or scared or moving quickly, they slip into their base lizard brains and grab whatever name is there and easiest; it takes some people a long time to catch on. Then there are those who want you to know they don't respect you. They don't accept the "new" you. They won't call you by your name and in fact will deadname you on purpose because their religion may tell them that if they don't, they'll be condoning something they don't agree with. Let me pause for a moment. There are other reasons why someone may be deadnaming another person on purpose, aside from religious reasons, but for those doing it out of a

---

30 Wikipedia: The Free Encyclopedia, September 2024, https://en.wikipedia.org/wiki/Deadnaming.

devotion to their religion, specifically institutions that seem to prioritize narrow interpretations of biblical text, I'd challenge them to think long and hard about that. Abram to Abraham, Sarai to Sarah, Saul to Paul, and the list goes on and on. These name changes we accept as part of a new beginning for these characters, and we should do the same for our trans and nonbinary sons, daughters, children, family, and friends.

When all is said and done, most people aren't doing it on purpose. They aren't doing it to be disrespectful or to show me that they don't accept who I am. However, that doesn't mean it doesn't hurt. As a trans person, coming out is saying, "Here I am, this is me, see me!!!" But when I'm deadnamed, the first thing I think is, *What am I doing wrong? Am I not presenting feminine enough? Why don't they see me?*

It makes me feel like I'm not good enough. That if I try harder then they'll see. But if the onus is on me to make them see, then I'll start doing things that aren't me to make them see. I'll start wearing heavier makeup. I'll start dressing like a 1950s housewife, feminine to the hilt, changing my mannerisms more, changing my behavior to meet expectations for the as-long-as crowd. And yes, I like to dress up sometimes and I wear makeup, but if I start doing these things to get other people to see me as a woman, I'll lose myself in the process. And after finding myself after all these years, that would be a crying shame.

So, now when someone deadnames me, I simply say, "It's Nia." If they haven't done it on purpose, they'll apologize profusely, and most likely have already corrected their mistake themselves before I had to. If they did do it on purpose, they won't care what I say. And for those people, unfortunately, I've had to say goodbye for now. Out of respect for myself. Out of respect for my journey. Out of respect for them and their choices. When I ask to be called by my name, just as I call everyone else by their name, and that isn't honored, I have to hold a boundary. And when people have said to me, "We just won't call you anything," I've also had to say no. Even dogs have names. This means possibly losing friends and loved ones, because I deserve to feel human, honored, loved, and respected.

Boundary making in this way is important for all of us. When we change and grow and present our new self to the world, we deserve respect. Other people may want to continue to see us as the person they knew before and continue to treat us that way, but it isn't fair. It isn't fair to the hard work and dedication that we've put into finding out who we are. And it isn't fair to them to continue in a relationship where they think we're something we're not.

Just like the journey my grandpa took over the seas, to a new land, to make a new life, I have journeyed many years to find myself, arriving at a new land, making a new life. And just like him, I've changed my name to signal a new start. My name is Nia, and I love who I am.

Rumors

It was February 2019. Things felt out of control, as transitioning genders is wont to do. Remember that trip that I took all the way to Mexico with a friend to find myself? I had only hung out with my friend Tree twice at that point, but they were planning their own trip, and I needed a trip, away from everything that was going on, so I texted. I said, "So this is weird, but the trip you described that you were taking is exactly what I'm looking for. I'm not looking to horn in on your trip, but that weekend works for me too and I was wondering if you'd be willing to tell me what airlines you booked? I promise if I do it, you won't see me (Laughing emoji). The ocean and layover in the mountains sound perfect."

Bold move on my part, inviting myself on a near stranger's cross-country trip.

Their response to me, someone they had just met, was this: "Hah! I was just working on my bike for a couple of hours and thinking damn, why doesn't Nia just join me for my trip?? That sounds perfect and so life-giving—but I didn't want you to feel pressure if you want the alone experience. Honestly, I'd love for you to join all the way through Baja if you're interested!"

My text back was the beginning of a lifelong friendship. I replied, "'When and where are you going?' she said, trying not to sound too eager (laugh cry emoji)."

We agreed to do this together, along with another soon-to-be friend who I hadn't yet met. I would go alone first, indeed needing time to myself. After arriving in Denver, I met yet another friend (another trans friend from my graduating high school class of thirty-six) who I hadn't seen in a long time and headed up into the mountains to the hippy hot springs on the Orient Land Trust.

It was an amazing experience. At age thirty-five, I hadn't traveled alone before and been free to do whatever I wanted. During my time at the hot springs, I solidified through much personal meditation and contemplation that I am a woman. I knew I was trans before that trip, but I now knew I was going to use she/her pronouns. A momentous moment that felt huge, and like nothing at all at the same time. After the trip to the hot springs, I made my way back down the mountains and headed to Phoenix.

Once in Phoenix, I met a dear friend who I hadn't seen in ten years. We had breakfast and caught up. At the time, I had been out to my family (parents and siblings) for about four months. I had been on hormones for six months. And although I got my first feminine-styled haircut for the trip, I was not feminine looking. Which meant I had the joy of coming out to my friend out of the blue, with my newly pierced ears being the only things to cue him in on my news. It was the first time I had done this, and at the time it was difficult, although he responded with generosity, despite our shared evangelical Christian bond.[31]

After breakfast I met up with Tree and one of their friends.

"Hi, Nia, my name is Dan." The stranger stuck out their hand as we met up at the car rental facility on our way to Mexico.

"Hi, Dan, nice to meet you," I said as I shook the hand of my new friend, realizing this was the first time I had met someone new with my new name. This person, a friend of a friend, had no chance of deadnaming me, because they didn't know my old name. They just knew me, Nia.

Like much of this sojourn into the mountains, down into the desert and down to the Gulf of California, this one small moment was freeing.

---

31 Since then, I've come to love coming out to old friends. It really is a fun activity for me to show up and say, "Hi, this is me!"

It was the first of many encounters where I would introduce myself by my new name.

It was one of the best experiences of my life. We hiked and swam and ate some amazing tacos, burritos, and ceviche as we experienced the small Mexican towns.

I can hardly say the trip was uneventful in that it was so life-giving and just what I needed at that point in my journey; however, it was pretty uneventful by most measures. No snafus, no missed flights, no problems in Mexico (Tree speaks Spanish), and everything went off without a hitch. But then I came home.

When I returned, I started to hear some interesting rumblings about the reasons for my trip. If you're not familiar with evangelical prayer (gossip) chains, they go something like this: "Oh, did you hear (deadname) is having some issues? I think he is having a crisis of faith. Please pray for him. Oh, how do I know? Well, you didn't hear it from me, but he just left town looking for something." That was what was getting back to me, although I came to find out later that the actual rumor was much more specific and direct than that, and it was started by a relative.

But I first need to go back, before the trip, to something that I posted on social media. Before you scold me for stirring up trouble, let me explain.

My wife had gotten a new tattoo on her finger, a peace sign inside of a heart, and she had posted on Instagram about how it served as a reminder to her to always be present with Peace and Love. Someone said something passive aggressively about the tattoo with emojis to back it up. At the time, I wasn't a fan of emojis or their use in passive aggressive online diatribes. So to counter, I pulled up my emoji keyboard and responded to the comment by hitting random emojis over and over until I felt I had made my point to convey support for my wife as well as my anger toward passive aggressive emojis (I know, I know, talk about passive aggression). I ended up posting, Heart x5, Fire x3, Winky Face, Knife,

Banana. My hatred for emojis equaled my own passive aggressive emoji soup.

However, not everyone saw it that way, reading something into the emojis that clearly wasn't there. Can you guess which emojis my rumor-loving relative homed in on?

Yep. Knife, Banana.

Below is the full rumor as told to me by other family members who weren't sure of its authenticity and passed it along to me for verification, my clarifying brackets added.

Deadname [Nia], declaring [being] himself [herself] transgender, immediately [four months after coming out], hopped on a plane to Mexico [Denver]. Once there, he [she] sought an illicit, back-alley sex change [gender confirmation surgery] operation. Bringing along of course one of his [her] closest friends [we'd only hung out twice] because of course, they used to be a reporter for a newspaper [the only true part of the rumor], and they were doing a story on trans people and wanted to document the entire surgery [WTF?].

Upon hearing this, I lost my mind.

"Uh, what? My own relative said what? How could...? Why did...? Who the HELL HAS HEARD THIS? BUT IT ISN'T TRUE!"

In hindsight, I see how someone with a pathological proclivity for conspiracy theories might read something into this, as I did leave out my wife's response to the banana knife emoji and my response to her response. Katie, not knowing what my emojis meant, responded with, "I feel like the knife and banana are overkill... or maybe I don't know something that you do? Laughing Emoji."

My response: "Oh if you only knew."

Although my wife knew I was trans at the time, my playful response had no understanding of how these emojis, when typed consecutively, may imply I want to cut off my penis. So, while my sense of humor may have been partly to blame for the start of this rumor, I 99 percent blame the evangelical prayer (gossip) chain.

And while I truly do understand people's curiosity about trans individuals' bodies, it's really none of their business. And on top of that, if you are going to join in the rumor sharing, then stop and ask yourself, "If I wanted to verify this information, would I ask this person directly?" If the answer is no, don't spread the rumor. If the answer is yes, then ask the question. What's the worst that can happen? We tell you to get lost? Yeah, that's the worst that can happen. But often, if you're a friend or someone who is genuinely seeking to understand trans people, I'll talk to you about it. Although not all trans people feel the same.

As I move through life, I now understand some people will create safe spaces, and some people will create spaces meant to be void of safety on purpose. We see this more and more in the political landscape, which should be serving the people instead of hurting us.

Unfortunately, this wasn't the first time, and it wasn't the last, that unsubstantiated rumors flew and people talked about me behind my back. A few years ago, a new friend confirmed that he was on the staff of a church, across town from the church I was at when I came out, and his pastor called a staff meeting—to discuss me. Fortunately, though, I now better understand myself and (typically) can laugh and wonder how people have so much time on their hands, as I release the rumor into the air.

Some are harder than others, but because most have circulated on the evangelical prayer (gossip) chain and are about my physical body, they're easy for me to ignore.

But seriously, stop talking about our bodies behind our backs, even if the rumors are true.

My Body

Bodies are fascinating. Did you know that one person has almost sixty thousand miles of blood vessels in their body? That's more than twice around the earth! I also just learned that human stomach acid is so strong, it can dissolve a razor blade. In science class, I learned that each person sheds an average of almost fifty pounds of skin in their lifetime. The one that always gets me scratching my head though, is that humans share 50 percent of their genes with bananas. (This fact is not very appealing.)

With how complex we are as humans, it's no wonder then that many of us have complicated emotional and physical relationships with our bodies. As a transgender individual, these issues are unavoidable. I did a pretty good job of avoiding them though until I was in my mid-thirties. My love for being active as well as being outdoors helped ground me in my body, even if much of it was in gender-specific activities such as little league and church basketball (definitely no girls allowed there). Even though puberty quickly opened my eyes to the fact that things were not progressing how I'd hoped, I was able to hide that part of myself away quickly. I hid the female side of me that wasn't welcome in the world I suddenly found myself in, one where I had to act like a man. So I hid her away, a treasure only to be found later by the person who had buried her (see my book, *The Story of Nib*).

It was a weird mix of not really hating my own body, but as someone gendered one way, just wanting to be in a different body—anyone else's (like every girl I ever saw or met growing up). I knew this was impossible, and if it was in fact possible, it would be something God frowned upon (or so I was told). Every environment I was in, evangelical Christian school, evangelical Christian church, evangelical Christian home, all told me explicitly that God made man and woman, there is nothing in between these two binaries, and anything that pretends to be something other than one of these two is an imposter.[32] My environment told me a lot of other things about gender and bodies too, mostly creating dynamics in male-female relationships that were not healthy by any stretch of the imagination.

For some of us, parts of our body literally protrude out into the world. Before you go there, I'm talking about arms obviously. We can let people know, "Hi, I see you!" by waving our hands. Our arms and hands can be used to construct sandcastles, monuments, buildings, cities, and nations. Even our words go out from our lips to say, "I love you," to a friend or lover. Our bodies, desperately wanting to survive over the course of millions of years, have spun up consciousness and a complex brain to assist in survival and to further our projection outward.

With all the good and marvelous things our bodies can do, like everything that exists, we must take the good with the bad. We can use our hands not only to wave but also to say, "Hey, fuck off!" out of the open window of a car on the highway. We can build wonderful masterpieces but also use weapons of mass destruction to destroy nations, cities, buildings, monuments, sandcastles, and other people. Out of the same mouth that can project love, we can send words that cut someone down so far that they don't get back up. Our brain can, at the same time, appreciate the beauty of a sunset while torturing us from the inside through depression and anxiety. Together, we are a complex species, each individual relating to their body in different ways.

For me, I've always longed to protrude out into the world a little less in some ways and a little more in others (yes, you can go there now). But

---

32 Austen Hartke's book *Transforming* (Westminster John Knox Press, 2018) is a great primer on the in-between, dawn and dusk, and everything else.

before I talk about my own body dysphoria in length, I should make two disclaimers. First, a content warning as I will be talking about body parts and my satisfaction/dysphoria with various parts. This may be uncomfortable for some trans individuals, especially those who don't have access to the medical care they desire. Second, I am aware that many of us trans folx[33] don't talk about this type of thing out in the open for a very specific reason. We don't want it to be used against us. We're all varied and diverse, and there isn't one specific way to be trans. You can be a fully content trans woman with a penis. You can be a fully content trans man with a vagina. You can be any and every combination of every gender, sex, body part, and chromosomal makeup you can think of. The problem here isn't that this is complex, although it is. The problem is that society at large is binary. Men's and women's clothes sections, men's and women's restrooms. Act like this if you're a man, act like that if you're a woman. You either have these body parts or those body parts. If a trans or nonbinary person doesn't fit easily into a narrative, it becomes difficult. The narrative around biological sex and gender only gets more complicated when trans people talk about our bodies, the good and the bad, and if taken out of context, it makes any negative narrative surrounding trans individuals that much easier to propagate.

All of that said, I think it is important to discuss, out in the light of day, the body struggles that some trans people go through. I know I've learned from others' stories, and I hope my story will illuminate some of the mystery surrounding trans bodies so that we will be more accepted, treated less like a curiosity and something to be feared and vilified. Also, I want to be clear that I am voluntarily sharing my story. That doesn't mean you can come up to me, without a relationship with me, and ask me about my body. You shouldn't do that to anyone. Period.

Okay, so where do I begin?

---

33 Spelled with an X, folx can be used as a way to explicitly signal the inclusion of groups commonly marginalized.

It was a dark and stormy night, as I squeezed my way out into the world. As I took my first screaming gasps of air, the doctor pronounced, "It's a boy!"

Usually a story starting out like this is meant to be hyperbole, but in this case, it works. And while I don't exactly remember what happened, and definitely don't remember what the weather was like (although Google tells me it was a nice high of sixty-three with no precipitation), it's pretty safe to say I was pronounced a boy upon arrival. This is what we call assigning a sex at birth. I was assigned male at birth (AMAB), while some people are assigned female at birth (AFAB). This is done solely by looking at genitals. If the genitals of a child cannot be determined to be a penis or a vulva explicitly, which happens more often than you think, many times a doctor or a combination of doctors and parents will choose which gender to assign, which can be extremely damaging to a person in the long run. And while more and more light is being shed each day on the atrocities and forced surgeries that intersex individuals face, I will leave that conversation for another day and to someone who is intersex.

I don't think most of us trans individuals blame our parents for assigning us to a biological sex based on what they saw in that moment. Many times when people hear "I was assigned male at birth," they assume we're angry about it. This happens because we typically say it in the context of not being happy about the sex we were assigned at birth. Our unhappiness, though, doesn't assign blame. Parents don't know any better. Hell, I assigned all my kids' sexes at birth. You have to. Society is set up that way. The thing is, when you know better, you do better. So, my kids are assigned male or female until they tell me otherwise.[34] When some of us talk about being AMAB or AFAB with some anger in our voice, it's because our parents assumed (and many still do) that this

---

34 I first heard Glennon Doyle use this language on her podcast, *We Can Do Hard Things*.

assignment is immutable and there are no allowances for change. This is clearly not the case.

But for me, in 1982, I was assigned a sex so my parents could check off any forms they needed to fill out for their zero-day-old child. Unfortunately, I was assigned the wrong sex. This kicked off a thirty-five-year fight with my body. My parents, everyone around me, the world in fact (and all the forms) were telling me I was one sex, while my body felt like it should be a different one.

This is where sex and gender start to get conflated. Let me paraphrase scientist and friend, Cade Hildreth, founder of BioInformant.com.

Biological sex refers to a "constellation of traits," not just external genitals and secondary sex characteristics like breasts, facial or body hair, body shape, and pitch of voice, but many traits which we can't see, including chromosomes, hormones, internal genitalia, genes, and brain structure.[35]

And even though in our society we usually say the mix of these traits amounts to either a man or a woman, in fact none of these traits alone or in combination fits neatly into a binary. While we organize our cultures with these dichotomous categories and have created our legal system around it, there are many combinations of these biological traits that exist on a spectrum, from male to intersex to female and everything in between. This occurs in humans and throughout the animal kingdom. (Some animals we know and love actually change sex as adults, including five hundred species of fish, like the beloved clown fish.)

Gender, on the other hand, is a social identity or group of identities organized around biological sex. It includes gendered behavior, gender roles, gender expression, and much more. Gender also exists on a wide

---

35 More information can be found in Cade's article, "Gender Spectrum: A Scientist Explains Why Gender Isn't Binary" (November 8, 2024) at https://cadehildreth.com/gender-spectrum/. Another great resource is Julia Serano's book *Whipping Girl* (Seal Press, 2016).

spectrum and is very much influenced by language and culture, with different cultures having different words for more than just two genders.

You can even see with these definitions that gender and biological sex become commingled very quickly. That is why I personally like to talk about *gender/sex*, a relatively new term I first read about in *Discover* magazine. Sari van Anders, a social neuroendocrinologist at Queen's University in Kingston, Canada, coined the term with this definition:

> The concept of 'gender/sex' (van Anders & Dunn, 2009) refers to whole people (women, men, genderqueer, etc.) who reflect gender socialization and evolved [biological] sex. Typically, human biology focuses on sex (femaleness, maleness, maybe sex-diversity) while sociocultural research focuses on gender (femininity, masculinity, maybe gender-diversity). Gender/sex expresses a more empirically accurate entanglement in queer and scientific terms.[36]

I do think it's nearly impossible to talk about a whole person and separate the concepts of gender and sex. That being said, I'll continue using terms I feel are appropriate as I go, to make this easier to read.

So, where was I—oh yes, the beginning of the thirty-five-year fight with my body. To be fair, it wasn't a full thirty-five years. I knew what gender people were telling me I was as a kid, and while it didn't feel exactly right, it didn't rub up against my bodily reality that often because I hadn't yet experienced all the joys of puberty. Once that happened though, the fight began in earnest.

While I was mostly comfortable in my skin before my body started to develop, all of a sudden, I wasn't. I got hair in all the wrong places. My chest didn't grow like my brain thought it should. And of course, I protruded into the world further than I would have liked. I started to

---

36 Allison Whitten, "Untangling Gender and Sex in Humans," *Discover*, July 23, 2020, https://www.discovermagazine.com/health/untangling-gender-and-sex-in-humans.

daydream about having different body parts. It wasn't like I thought I could have them; it was just something I needed to do to quiet my brain. But it rarely worked. In fact, that's why I, like many others, felt like I had to come out when I did. As you go on in years, you just keep thinking about it more, and by the time I was in my mid-thirties, I was spending enormous amounts of time and energy hiding what I now realize was my body's pull to transition. Deflecting thoughts at the supermarket, "What if this checkout clerk knows my secret?" "Can the grocery bagger tell I'm different?" Eventually, it became too much. The mental energy and the physical exhaustion from hiding myself literally was killing me.

I wasn't whole and I knew it. Once I figured out how I wasn't whole, continuing down the road of unwholeness was so painstakingly difficult.

When it came to my body, before I started to transition, my dysphoria felt very generalized. I'd look into the mirror, and although I was fine with the guy I saw, it wasn't me. I wanted the world to see me, and I wanted to see me too. For me, the first step to overcoming body dysphoria was understanding and admitting that I was trans. And to break free of all the energy put into hiding from myself and others, I had to get to specifics about my dysphoria.

A quick detour for those making the argument that therapists can convince people that they're transgender, or that we the transgender army are brainwashing kids to think they're transgender (good for you if you hold this belief and made it this far!). Being transgender, uncovering that someone has a transgender identity, does not rear its head as a solution to someone's potential stress and discomfort unless they are actually trans. Those who are cisgender (alignment of their internal and external sense of gender) cannot be convinced to break that alignment. My favorite analogy comes from Julia Serano, paraphrased below.

If your internal sense of self (Serano calls this subconscious sex) and what you present to the world (conscious or physical sex) are the same, you wouldn't experience any distress.[37] And in fact, you would never consider transitioning. It would cause distress if you thought about transitioning. We know this because if this weren't the case, cisgender people would transition for periods of time for different reasons, maybe to be an actor or to go undercover on a journalistic assignment, submerging themselves into their work. Playing a part or going undercover may be options, but no one ever chooses actual physical transition for these types of things because it would throw off a person's aligned subconscious and conscious sex.

If I asked you how much money I could give you to get you to transition, if you're cisgender, most likely your answer is no amount of money could make you transition. You'd be more likely to play the Squid Games before transitioning to get out of debt. If you did transition, you would feel out of alignment. This is how I used to feel every day. I was always in distress because my subconscious and conscious sex didn't align. To the point where I would pay money to transition to get them to align. And I did.

My body, before transition, was seen as hard, masculine, and tough. I even leaned toward the masculine for other things. Masculine clothes, masculine haircut, masculine mannerisms. My generalized dysphoria, though, wanted to see myself in the mirror as more feminine, whatever that meant.

Once I realized and I admitted to myself that I was transgender, my dysphoria became more specific. I think when the possibility of changing things about my body became a reality, I started seeing all the masculine things I never liked about myself. I had to sort through what society was telling me I should be if I were to be seen as a woman, and what my body was asking of me.

The first thing I knew was that I wanted to get on hormones. For people assigned male at birth, transitioning to female, there are options

---

37 This and many more helpful concepts are in Serano's *Whipping Girl*, a must-read if you like science.

for hormones. These typically include estrogen, testosterone blockers, and progesterone. Some people do one of these, some do all three, and some trans women don't do any of them for any number of reasons. All these hormones have potentially different effects on the body. I ended up on all three over the course of eighteen months. Let me tell you how I obtained these hormones. Contrary to popular belief, it wasn't easy; they aren't just handing them out.

I first met with my doctor for a thorough evaluation. He asked me for a note from my therapist. Once he had her thoughts on my gender dysphoria, he went through some questions with me. These were questions based on the criteria from the American Psychiatric Association's latest *Diagnostic and Statistical Manual (DSM-5)* to determine if I experienced gender dysphoria. I met the criteria, and he started me on graduated doses of estrogen and testosterone blockers. Over the course of a year, he gradually increased the dosage. In that time, my body started changing. I experienced markedly softer skin. My sex drive decreased to a level that I felt more comfortable with. Fat and muscle started to move around in my body, making my hips and booty bigger and wider and my arms and chest less muscular. And speaking of chest, wow, did it hurt. It hurt as my breast buds sprang to life. It was a second puberty as a thirty-five-year-old after all.

Once I generally started to see my body as more feminine, more specific things started to stick out to me. I didn't like my body hair. My hands were too big. My face wasn't feminine enough. My voice was too deep. Then there was that pesky penis. All these things can be worked on through therapy and surgery. All of them are very expensive, and for all trans people, including myself, we must weigh the costs—monetarily, physically, mentally, and emotionally—of these changes and surgeries, and decide if they are for us and what their actual effect on countering any dysphoria might be. And what if any dysphoria comes from the way society tells me I should look now that I am seen as a woman? It's complicated.

This is a struggle we all deal with. Who we should be, what we should look like laid out for us by a society that likes certainty and likes us to meet expectations. Whether I should get a breast augmentation, nose job, tummy tuck, and vaginoplasty aren't questions just trans people are asking, but questions cis women ask themselves all the time. They, too, must figure out if it's societal expectations they are trying to live up to or a deep desire to feel more like themselves.

I know my relationship with my body will always be complicated, but the more and more comfortable I get inside it, the more I learn to trust it. And the more I learn to trust it, the more I will lean in when she tells me what she needs. We used to not be on speaking terms, but now that we've reconciled, we try to talk every chance we get. And what is she saying to me right now? *About that 20/20 special we saw so long ago . . .*

(Sex) Changes

"You're going to feel a little cold," the nurse said as she leaned over me, suddenly coming into my frame of view from above.

"Count backward from ten," she continued. "We're on the move."

As I felt the motion of the bed rolling down the hall, I tried to concentrate on my task.

Ten, nine, eight, sleven, sax . . . fh . . .

The fluorescent lights of the hallway flickered, and everything was dark.

I opened my eyes slowly, trying to get the room to come into focus, but it wasn't working. Had I gone blind? Through the blurriness, I noticed a heart monitor and could make out the large number that was recording my breaths per minute. It read twelve. I started breathing in slowly and out slowly, counting to six on each inhale and exhale, slowly controlling the number on the monitor until it was down to 5.5, the ideal number of breaths per minute according to the book *Breath* by James Nestor, which I had just finished reading.[38] In and out, in and out, for two hours, until my vision finally started to return. I sat up, looking for someone to talk to. Was I okay? Was I different now? That remained to be seen.

They're called gender confirmation surgeries (GCS) or gender affirmation surgeries (GAS). These are a group of surgeries often used by transgender

---

38 James Nestor, *Breath: The New Science of a Lost Art* (Riverhead Books, 2020).

individuals that help us become on the outside the person we already see ourselves as on the inside. Most of the time when people talk about GCS and GAS surgeries, they're referring to what is colloquially known as bottom surgery (a vaginoplasty/labiaplasty for AMAB patients and a phalloplasty for AFAB patients). Other than bottom surgery though, there are all types of other gender affirming surgeries. There's breast augmentation (BA) and chest masculinizing surgeries (top surgery). There is facial feminization surgery (FFS) and voice feminization surgery. And while these surgeries are used by trans people, they're commonly used by cis women and men as well. A cis woman wanting breast augmentation uses GAS, as does a trans woman wanting the same surgery. Even a billionaire wanting a hair transplant uses gender affirming surgery.

Either way, the main surgery people think about when they think about trans surgeries, is bottom surgery. It could be because our society at large, including our religious society, is obsessed with genitals. We've set up all of society along a binary. What genitals you have determines which bathrooms and locker rooms you can use, which sports teams you can play on, which sections of the mall you should shop in, and on and on it goes. No matter that no one checks genitals before you go into these spaces. It's just on the honor system I guess.

More and more trans people are forgoing surgeries because they don't feel like they need to meet a binary that society has set up, especially if their internal sense of self isn't harmed by keeping their factory parts. For me, however, my subconscious sex was strong. I certainly could have lived without bottom surgery, but I was at a point where I needed it to lessen my dysphoria. For some people, when they decide to transition, they have it all planned out.[39] I know people who didn't come out until they had the whole two-, three-, five-, or ten-year plan. Coming out, socially transitioning,

---

39 Again, I want to clarify that being transgender isn't a choice. However, I call transitioning a decision because trans people should be in control and make their own decisions about when, where, and how to transition, or not to transition at all because of circumstances. And any way we decide to transition or not, we're still a valid trans person.

getting on hormones, surgery one, surgery two, surgery three. While this is helpful for them, I've struggled to be that methodical and have had to stop and listen more to what my emotions (or maybe my Knot) are revealing to me as I go. For someone like me who grew up in a religious context where emotions were suppressed and rational thinking criticized, I've had to take an ear-to-the-ground approach, taking life moment by moment, listening to my body for what comes next.

My therapist once told me I would know what I needed to do when I needed to do it, and she was right. Once my dysphoria got so bad, I first came out to myself and my spouse. It relieved some pressure, but that pressure soon began to build back up only a few months later. I decided that hormones might help relieve some pressure, so I got on a testosterone blocker and estrogen. This was super helpful, but then I started having panic attacks because, at the time, I was starting to live two lives—one where I was out to myself and my wife and one where I was not out to others—that were separating more and more. After three months on hormones, I came out to my family on a whim, and my plan was to wait and see how much pressure was relieved and how long it would last. But coming out to family only made things worse, it created more of a chasm between who I knew myself to be and the life I was living every day. And the life I was living every day, the life I had lived since I was born, was starting to make me realize, I needed to do more.

After I came out to my family, I wanted to transition socially, at work, and at church, and do it right away. In hindsight, I should have come out to everyone right then. That is what I needed, and no one should have told me differently. But I was in a leadership position at church, and I let the other leaders determine the process and timing for when I should come out. When I finally did come out at church, I came out at work one month later and was completely socially transitioned one year after I initially came out to myself that day in therapy.[40]

---

40 Social transitioning is not a medical process, but the process of expressing and living as another gender in everyday life.

I wasn't sure what would be next, because up to that point, I had been focused on merging my two lives. To the extent that I succeeded, my dysphoria was greatly reduced, but it came with a whole host of other societal anxieties.

After being out for a while, the dysphoria once again returned.[41] First around my facial and body hair. I worked through it with over twenty-five hours of electrolysis and forty-plus laser hair removal sessions, and once I felt comfortable that no one could see the remnants of a possible manly goatee, my dysphoria shifted again. (Again, many people may not feel the need to fit into this binary anymore as hairy women and hairless men become more acceptable in our society.)

Eventually, the dysphoria pointed down below, and I scheduled bottom surgery.

The gatekeeping criteria that need to be met for gender confirmation surgery are even more rigorous than the bar for getting on hormones, as it should be. Typically, a person has to be living as the opposite gender in society for at least twelve months. Some say there should be no gates or hoops to jump through to get medications and surgeries if you identify as trans. Others, such as the conservative evangelical right which is now a political policy-making machine, say that because any and all people might accidentally transition, people should have to fight for the right to transition or not be allowed to transition at all. Fortunately, the US medical community follows the World Professional Association for Transgender Health (WPATH) standards of care that attempts a middle ground.[42] These standards can sometimes be hotly debated within the trans community, but they include criteria which need to be met to be prescribed hormones or have a surgery.

---

41 LGBTQ+ people are never fully out. We come out to new people all the time, sometimes daily. Sometimes we have choice in the matter and sometimes we don't, but coming out is a constant in many of our lives.

42 More information on the specific WPATH standards and criteria can be found at https://www.wpath.org/soc8.

Many activists say there should be nothing like this, and trans folks should be in control of their own healthcare. And while I agree that trans individuals need to be able to control their own healthcare, WPATH seems like reasonable criteria to meet before being prescribed life-altering medication. In addition to criteria like these, all the risks are outlined in the WPATH manual (currently 120 pages). Again, good trans healthcare requires patients to know the risks.

While it's true that irresponsible medical care for trans people happens, it is very rare. What often creates a scenario for poor care is conservative legislation. The "detransition" movement pushed by conservative politics in the US isn't an accurate depiction of trans people and access to medical care. To say that a medical professional forced medication or surgery on me or anyone else would be disingenuous. As a trans woman, I had to meet the WPATH criteria to get medication, having a therapist sign off. Then I had to live life as a woman, socially, for at least twelve months, before then going through the hoops to schedule surgery, including getting two mental health therapists' signatures. I then waited almost two years after it was scheduled before that surgery even took place. If anyone goes through this process and regrets what they've done after surgery, transitioning back to their previous gender, they have missed some big opportunities to do the internal work it takes to live an authentic life. I say this from experience.[43]

I took the opportunity to do the work those months and years since coming out publicly. I lived in society as a transgender woman for two-plus years. I've had countless therapy sessions, hoping to find something else that was the "cause" of my dysphoria, something like my father didn't pay enough attention to me or I didn't play with enough trucks growing up. But since those things don't cause people to be trans,

---

43 Gender affirmation surgery regret rates have been studied and are less than one percent, which is much less than regret rates for most other surgeries studied. *American Journal of Surgery*, August 2024, www.americanjournalofsurgery.com/article/S0002-9610(24)00238-1/abstract.

I thought maybe my therapist could help me find something, anything else that would ease my discomfort. (Spoiler: when you're actually trans, it's hard to find one of these causes because they aren't there; you're just trans.)

It's been a hard road to get to surgery. There have been many hurdles and challenges, but here I am. At the door of the matrix. Scheduled for surgery tomorrow.

Yikes. Saying that out loud is emotional. So many emotions.

I'm excited. I'm nervous. I'm scared.

Typically, we just hear about the excited emotion. As trans people, we're expected to talk about our excitement. Our excitement to have our bodies match our brains, our excitement to (hopefully) be more accepted by society at large. But society almost demands we only talk about our excitement and not all our feelings about it. After all, we who were born this way, from day one, should be nothing but excited about such a change.

But this kind of change is life altering, and as such, it's also terrifying! There are all sorts of thoughts. What if something goes wrong? What if recovery is too difficult? What if my sexual function disappears? What if I pee sideways afterward? (Yes, this is sometimes a side effect of the surgery, though it can be addressed.) So many concerns, but we need to put on a happy face, not nervous at all, because people think this is the most exciting thing that's ever happened to us. For most of us though, it's scary as well as exciting. Many have to go through it alone, which is even worse.

Fortunately, I have a great support team. And if I've learned anything about being a trans person so far, it's that your support team is everything. It doesn't take away all the fear, but it does help amp up the excitement when you have a group of people by your side cheering you on.

So, here's what I'm going to do. I'm going to stop making observations about it for now and get back to it on the other side, when the surgery is over. Hopefully less scared, more excited.

I made it! Six days post gender confirmation surgery! Can you tell? Is my writing completely different? I bet it's just seeping with confidence as I write from my hospital bed.

Like so much of my transition, there's nothing different about me after this surgery, and at the same time, everything is different.

They just took my factory parts and turned them inside out to create something new, something integrated. Say what???

It's hard to describe what I've been feeling the last few days. Normally post-surgery feelings are not something we talk about in the trans community. Again, we don't want the trans-hating social media talking heads of the world to get hold of anything we say and use it to further hate on and marginalize us. If we do discuss it though, the feelings are always couched in a positive light. "Best decision I've ever made." "I am 467 percent happier now!" "It's like I've always had this body part."

Let me just say, it is not like I've always had this body part. And I want to talk about what I am really feeling. Not just the good parts.

First, do I regret it?

No. I don't regret it.

Am I happy?

Yes. The overwhelming feeling I have, though, is best described as hesitancy. There's a bit of fear. (Will the pain last forever? Will I ever be able to walk like anything other than a penguin again?)

There's a bit of unknown (How do I pee? How do I recover during the next six weeks without being able to sit down? What will it look like?).

And there were a few surprises. I really didn't expect it to feel like nothing has changed while also feeling like everything has changed. I don't feel like I've always had this body part ... and at the same time I do, because I have.

All that leaves me feeling hesitantly hopeful. My hope is that I'll be able to be fully excited about this down the road, but this is where I'm at now. Hesitantly hopeful. Concentrating on pooping, peeing, recovering from a major surgery that has me unable to sit. I am so glad I did it, but I'll get back to you and we'll see if I have any different feelings.

For now, I am so grateful to be able to do this. The access I have, the support team around me, I am glad to be alive in a time when there are more surgeons available, and good ones at that. It remains to be seen if I'll get any other surgeries down the road, but for now, me and my new labia need a nap.

I didn't anticipate continuing to write but felt like I needed to write down how my feelings are changing. I'm now fourteen days out from surgery, and the last fourteen days have been hard. Adjusting to a new body while getting back on hormones has left me depressed, overwhelmed with hot flashes, full of emotions that won't come out, and feeling like this change (the pain, not being able to sit down) will last forever.

Especially last week, it was hard to envision full healing taking place after a surgery like this. With the help of some friends and family though, who have been making me get out of bed and getting me outside into the sunlight, things feel better this week. Yes, my back hurts from lying around at ungodly angles (always less than 45 percent!), and yes, I'm still tired and depressed and eating a lot of my favorite candy, but things do feel better today. I've been trying to write for the past week and have been unable to until today. I'm told things will get better. My hope is that I'll look back on this time, even three months from now and say, "Wow, I was really blowing that out of proportion." Here's to a new normal.

It's been two and a half months now since my surgery. I had to write a brief addendum because—well, I wasn't blowing my experience out of proportion. I was very, very depressed. And the reason for it wasn't because I underwent gender confirmation surgery and regretted it. It was because my life was thrown into complete chaos. My independence was taken from me. My life experiences with my family were unavailable to me. I couldn't eat a meal with friends or even sit at the dinner table with my kids. For anyone who's had a major surgery or life-altering impairment, this sentiment may be familiar. For me, it was very acute because the healing period, the intense healing, is only about six weeks. I feel almost completely back to the way I was before the surgery. And I can very honestly now say, it was the best decision I've ever made.

Okay, one last entry. It's been three and a half years since I had my surgery. Every single day I look at my body in the mirror, I feel deep satisfaction and contentment. There are, of course, still things I want to change. I should exercise more and eat better, but the contentment I feel, the deep connection between my body and brain, is real and stronger than ever. It's something I could have never imagined before. It's a reason why gender affirming surgeries are so life-giving and should not be holistically banned.

I see now why people only talk about their surgery in hindsight and not while they're in the middle of it. But I think it's important to know, it's okay to be scared, depressed, and anxious.

Will I get more surgeries down the road? Time will tell. As trans people, we often view ourselves through our own lens as well as the lens of others. And these days, I care less what society sees, and care more about what I see as beautiful.

The Virtue of Freetles

It was a day that my life changed forever. It was 5:00 a.m., the day after I was released from the hospital following my gender confirmation surgery. I was staying with friends in Milwaukee, and I awoke to a dog barking furiously on the street. Now, I'd like to blame the dog for my truncated night of sleep, but it was more likely I wasn't sleeping well anyway because of having my genitals turned inside out.

It doesn't matter why I was awake though, just that I was. And I did what any good American does when they can't sleep, I got on social media. I'm not sure what took me to Facebook that morning (Instagram is normally my platform of choice), maybe it was divine intervention. Either way, there I was, scrolling through Facebook Marketplace, when my life changed forever.

I came across an ad for freeze-dried Skittles, also known as Freeties, by Freetles. I wasn't sure what these weird planetary-looking things were, but I knew I needed some. Did I mention I go gaga for candy? My love for most candies (Swedish Fish and anything gummy topping the list) combined with my love for trying new things, including candies, cereals, and soda (or pop if you're from Iowa), plus my absolute boredom from being pent up in the hospital for the previous six days (I had already signed up for grad school in the hospital, what else was left to do?) was a perfect confluence of events. I needed the Freetles, at the time one of the only freeze-dried Skittles on the market. I looked at the shipping time on Facebook Marketplace, seven to ten days. That wouldn't do, I might be gone and back home by the time they arrived.

So, I switched over to something even more American than social media, Amazon Prime.

I promptly discovered that Amazon carried all types of freeze-dried candies, and while freeze-dried taffy distracted me for a moment, I found the Freetles. To my absolute joy, if I ordered them in the next hour, they would be delivered *that day*! This was not a common occurrence where I came from in Des Moines, but in the big city of Milwaukee where my friends were, life moves faster I guess. My instant gratification nerve succumbed to the shipping markup, and I put in an order. A painstaking nine hours later and I was diligently waiting in the front room of my friends' house for my new temptation to arrive. At 2:00 p.m., my package arrived, and I wasted no time and dove in (I mean, I seriously had nothing else to do).

If you've ever tried Freetles, you'll understand, they are different. The appeal of a Skittle is the soft, chewy center, surrounded by an assortment of artificially colored candy shells (all which taste the same) infused with the scent of our favorite fruits. Freetles on the other hand are hard. They hurt to eat. In fact, if you're thinking of a Skittle when you eat one, you'll be sorely disappointed. Which I was. Now, I know what you're thinking. I said my life changed forever. It did, I promise. I just still didn't know it.

I spent another seven days with my friends, eating a few Freetles here and there between watching *The Godfather* movies, *The 40-Year-Old Virgin*, and *Dazed and Confused* for the first time. On the six-hour car ride home, I told my friend Kristin, who had picked me up, about my new purchase of Freetles. She made fun of my penchant for purchasing weird stuff, but then, as the candyphiles that we are, we started eating them. After a few, Kristin, in her infinite wisdom, suggested we suck on them like a lollipop instead of crunching down. This was the life-changing instruction I needed. We (mostly me) proceeded to eat the rest of the bag on the way home, Kristin having to hide them from me halfway through the ride because it was a fairly large bag, and I was supposed to be eating healthy after surgery. During an intense hot flash I was having (going off hormones before surgery resulted in menopause-like symptoms), she took the opportunity and grabbed the bag and flung them to the back of the car and out of reach for the rest of the ride. But when I got home, I found them and finished the bag that night. Over the course of the next few weeks while convalescing in my home, lying around on my back, I bought *ten more bags of Freetles.* I had to wait the standard two-day Amazon Prime waiting period for each bag, but I soon figured out my eating habits and ordered before I ever ran out.

Ya'll, I spent over a hundred dollars on freeze-dried Skittles in the span of a month. Yes, it was a problem. I've since understood Freetles to be a delicacy, to be enjoyed sparingly, but that's not the point of this story.

A few weeks into my Freetles Frenzy, Kristin texted and asked what I was doing. I told her I was writing, and she responded with, "What, a chapter on the virtue of Freetles?" While I was in fact writing about my feelings after bottom surgery, it got me thinking, there is something to be learned from Freetles.

When I backed out of this candy crazed moment in my life, I realized that freeze-dried Skittles can teach us a lot about trans people.

Even though I was so taken aback and initially uninterested in the Freetles because they were so different from Skittles, I have now come to understand, they are still Skittles. Even though their outside and their inside has been changed, they're made of the same stuff. They've undergone a transformation process.

When trans people come out, we first focus on the outward transformation. It throws people. "Who is this person I knew and loved?" they ask. Not understanding that the outside is just that, the outside.

Over time though, I've come to understand it wasn't only the outside that changed. The more Freetles I ate, I realized that they, too, are different on the inside. The candy DNA may be the same, but the way they are experienced is not. When someone comes out as transgender, much of our inside changes too.

We gain confidence. We live into the person we were always meant to be. If we have love and support around us, we may start to love life with a new vigor. We may try things we've never tried before. Our personality may seemingly change! I've seen so many people go from self-described introvert to major extrovert.

When a Skittle is freeze-dried, it blows up big and the inside is seen on the outside. Much the same happens to trans people when we start to live into who we were all along. We become more vulnerable and more of our inside can be seen along with our changing outside.

Even if you're not transgender, but someone who is open to change, growth, transition, and transformation, you can learn a lot about yourself here.

First, Freetles are freeze-dried. They don't spontaneously poof from small chewy Skittles to giant, rock-hard orbs. They undergo a process that took care to discover and create. In the same way, all of us, no matter where we are in our journey, trans or not, need support. We need love and careful handling as we are in the "freeze dryer" of life.

There also has to be an environment that shows us we are loved for who we are. My wife gave this to me, and when I came out, countless others handled me with care, understanding that I was going through a transformation, and understanding all the emotions that might come with that. Environment matters.

My wife and I started our Love in the Face nonprofit a few years after I came out for just this reason, to help churches, businesses, friends, and families cultivate environments that support trans people. And we hope it also helps LGBTQ+ people understand that they are worthy of putting themselves in these types of safe, nurturing environments.

Second, Freetles are an acquired taste. They aren't like Skittles. They're the same, but different now. We need to approach them differently. We need to interact with them in a different way. When we undergo transformation, we will be changed. We can act as though nothing is changing, but it is.

I've experienced this on both sides of the coin. I've had friends and family who've created that environment of safety for me say, "You're you, nothing changes." This sentiment is fabulous and music to a trans person's ears, but in reality, some things will change. You will see me as a woman and interact with me as such. On the other side of the coin, I've had people write very publicly about how they view me as a murderer of the person they knew. I don't need to point out how wrong and hurtful this is, but for the sake of our Freetles analogy, I will. I am still a human person, made of the same DNA, just different. Just because someone perceives me differently (which I've asked them to do by coming out) doesn't mean the person I used to be is gone. It means I have changed and grown. I've gone through the freeze dryer, and you will have to interact with me differently now as well. You can't just chomp down on me like the Skittle that I used to be; you now should savor the flavor of something new. And if you do, you just might find out that you've been missing something you didn't even know you were missing until you tried it.

This is one of the worst things about coming out to religious friends and family as transgender. Many folks have not even engaged with me after coming out because, somehow, having fun with me, hanging out with me, liking me, is seen as betraying their value system and worldview. But it's not. If you know your own values and you know yourself well, you can interact with and hang out with and have fun with anyone, and you can be self-differentiated enough to understand that person is not you and you are not that person (see Jesus Christ).

My good friend Jen illustrated how to do this so wonderfully. We were hanging out with a small group from church one day, when I came out to the group quite suddenly (per usual). I can't remember if I had planned it or not, or if I just needed to get it out there, but I did it. As soon as I said it, I could tell Jen was thrown. She asked some good questions, but I could tell this news did not fit with what she believed about the world. She was used to seeing me as a Skittle. I was asking her to see me as a Freetle. Our different realities were bumping into each other.

We parted ways that day, and I didn't hear from her for a few weeks. When she did reach out to me to follow up, she told me she had been uncomfortable when I came out. She didn't know why she was uncomfortable, so instead of projecting it onto me in the form of asking me to change or telling me I was a sinner, she went home to probe why it made her uncomfortable. After her own reflection, she worked through her own emotions surrounding my coming out, and instead of ejecting me out of her life because my story didn't fit into her worldview, she asked questions, and her view of the world became wide enough so both of our stories could be valued and fit together. Jen and I are still friends today. She didn't "compromise" her values, but she let love, her ultimate value, probe her other beliefs to open them up wider. Now me and my Freetle self can be a part of Jen's life.

Okay, I know I've taken this analogy way too far (I really, really like Freetles), but one last thing. My wife always says trans people are holy, and we even have a piece of art that says as much.[44] Katie says that transgender people allow others to experience something of the world, or of God, that was previously hidden. We open people's eyes to something completely new, something they may never have experienced without our presence. While I appreciate the high praise for trans people, I believe she's at least partially right.

I've seen it time and again with people I encounter. I do open something up inside of people. I'm your friendly neighborhood box buster. My very presence exposes something inside of people. Especially for those who aren't confident in their own Knowing—who haven't found out who they are—my presence seems to make people feel like it's me or them, there isn't room for both of us. In evaluating what they're going to

---

44 Jameson Malone is an artist who believes this as well and makes art that says as much. See www.jamiemalone.com.

do with this new piece of data that falls outside their worldview, they have a choice. Either fight like hell to tighten up the borders of their worldview box and make sure nothing gets in or out, or open up and expand to include me.

For many of my family and friends who are no longer in my life, it seems they believe that by including me, the Freetle, they somehow can't have Skittles anymore. But transformation can go both ways. When we find ourselves in a moment of transformation and growth, those around us can also transform and grow if necessary so we can continue forward together.

My hope is that if you have someone in your life who is in the middle of transition and growth and they are vulnerable with you in the future, that no matter what you think about the world, you'll allow that person to expand your box. If you do, I think you'll find out what you've been missing. And although you thought Skittles were the only way to go, life is so much better with both Skittles and Freetles.

Fear of Failure

I had another panic attack last night. I mean, why wouldn't I? It was the first night of a family vacation. What's better than crossing time zones and being up early due to a time change? Crossing time zones and sleeping hardly at all!

But seriously. Panic attacks suck. For those who get them, you know. For those who don't, there's no way to describe them in enough detail to make you feel them. They come in all shapes and sizes for different people. For me, my throat and nose close up (or feel like they are) making me unable to breathe, making my brain and body believe that not only is death imminent but also that I will get to stand by and watch the whole thing unfold.

My attacks are particularly alarming because up until the age of thirty-five, I'd never had one. Unlike many closeted LGBTQ+ people, before I came out, I never suffered from outright anxiety and depression that would look obvious to a psychiatrist. Looking back, however, I definitely had undiagnosed anxiety. We only know what we know.

When I did come out, I started to have full-blown, I-can't-breathe, I-think-I-need-to-go-to-the-hospital-right-now-or-I-will-die-a-painful-suffocating-death panic attacks. And they didn't start after I came out to myself. They didn't start after I came out to my wife and kids either. I did those things, lived my life, and even got on hormones for a while. Things were going really well.

The high anxiety started when I came out to people outside of my little family: first immediate family, then other extended family, and finally friends I'd known my whole life. The deluge of abandonment was so strong, and the attacks suddenly came on just as strong.

I didn't know what was happening the first time. I thought it was maybe something hormonal (it wasn't) or an allergic reaction. But after that first time, they came while in bed almost every night for a good month. It wasn't until I finally took that sojourn with my friend Tree across the country into Mexico that they finally started to slow down.

After years of therapy and anxiety medication, they've now mostly stopped. Not stopped suddenly like they'd come, but gradually fading away like a distant memory. There is no longer the threat of them hanging over me each night. For those who continue to live with them all the time, I will always have a great respect and much more empathy for how they live life with the constant threat.

But last night felt like déjà vu. And to be honest, it wasn't the first attack I've had in the last week. After not having any for over a year, clearly something new is going on. Last night was set off by a text I received, filled with more rumors. An alert in my brain went off, causing feelings of abandonment. That activation rubbed raw places inside me I didn't even realize were there. I also wasn't sure what the root of my recent panic attacks were until last night. You're reading this and going, obviously, it's abandonment. And you're partially right.

You see, my dad is in failing health. I haven't talked to him much in the last two years. Really not at all other than to continue to tell him I want to be in a relationship if he would just call me by my name. But even though he's had a bad heart for thirty-five years and was diagnosed with congenital heart disease five years back, the rumor is, my family is blaming me for his failing health. When I was young, he used to come to my church basketball games, fresh off his heart attack, and cheer me on. He couldn't get out on the court and play with me, but he encouraged me to be aggressive by paying me for each steal and each foul I made in the game. It was his way of getting out on the court with me.

Now, in my family blame-laden panic stew, I'm feeling abandonment and guilt. But I know intellectually and have done the work of internalizing deep down that I can't control the abandonment and the guilt isn't mine. So, I sat up last night, searching for what truly was at the root of all this. And you know what I found? That effen F-word. Failure. It's been so deeply ingrained in me, since I was a little kid—be a certain way, act like this, be a good Christian. Failure is not an option. And really, failure can come in all forms.

It's not just that I'm transgender (although most of my family would argue that's my biggest failure in their eyes); it's also that I'm no longer a Bible-thumping Christian (or maybe that is the biggest failure; chicken and the egg, I guess). And with failure to be a good Christian comes failure on a grand stage. The kind where there's only hell and eternal torment on the other side of death, waiting for you in your failure.

I've "failed" in this area. Since starting this journey, I have moved out of the Christian village entirely. Evangelical Christianity is still my home, and I will always have a fondness for it. I still speak the language and always will, but I have realized there are so many other places to travel out there, so many other languages to learn, and many more of them are much less harmful to my own health and well-being, as well as the health and well-being of those around me, than evangelical Christianity. I can't go home anymore. After a year without panic attacks, this one text, this one rumor, has brought all of this "failure" back to my door.

I've also "failed" to be a good son, husband, you-name-it label that someone else has put on me that I haven't lived up to. Society writ large asks all kinds of things from us. Katie recently told me about the concept of the *adaptive self*.[45] Our response to the things society is asking from us is the *adaptive self*. Many would call this the false self, the things we put on for whatever reason, typically because of the expectations of others, which

---

45 The adaptive unconscious is a term first coined by social psychologist Daniel Wegner in 2002 and describes the mechanism used by organisms to keep themselves alive.

then become our own expectations for ourselves. It's also referred to as our armor we put on to protect us. And while the false self makes sense as a phrase, calling it the adaptive self feels much more embodied to me.

As a kid, I created the self I needed to survive. I didn't want to fail, and I put on all sorts of masks, defined myself in all sorts of ways, only to please those around me. Those things eventually became my identity, pushing down my true self so far that I locked it away for twenty years. This is how personality and ego is built.

All the while, my adaptive self was building up this fear of failure. Most of it came from evangelical Christianity to begin with, but after a while my adaptive self took it on in a broader sense. I couldn't fail. Wouldn't fail. To the point that I wouldn't try anymore. I wouldn't try new things if I knew it could lead to failure.

As an example, I used to hate public speaking, for fear of failure. Blanking out in front of a group, forgetting my words, was a huge fear. So much so, when I enrolled in college classes, I perused the syllabus, then dropped the class if there was a large presentation in front of a group sometime during the semester. I missed out on some truly great learning experiences because of my fear of failure.

But fear of failure just continues to empower the adaptive self. I realized this after my panic attack subsided last night. Yes, I'm afraid of abandonment and I hold on to other people's guilt. And yes, I'm afraid that if I let go of those things, more of my adaptive self will fall away. It's scary to lose more of that self that kept me alive for so many years and is seen by others the way they want to see me. It's more of that loyal soldier that I discharged that night in New Mexico.

That adaptive self will continue to be replaced and rebuilt with my true Knowing if I let go of my fear of abandonment and the guilt that's been given to me. And although it's terrifying, I can't let go of my fear of abandonment and guilt until I let go of my fear of failure. I have to stop worrying about others' perception of me as a failure, a core part of my adaptive self, in order to move forward.

So last night, in the middle of my panic attack, I had a moment of clarity.

Is it worth it?

Is holding on to my adaptive self worth all this?

I'm using the word adaptive instead of false self because I want to honor the role my past self played in protecting me, keeping me insulated from death and conversion therapy. But holding onto something, even though it was beneficial in the past, is harming my future.

I don't want an intrusive text to be able to trigger me at random. I don't want to hold onto other people's emotions that aren't mine. I don't want to take on the expectations of those around me when they are counter to who I am as a person. I don't want to wake up in the middle of the night only to feel like I am suffocating to death. I want to free myself from the control of others. I want to release myself from my fear of failure. My true self deserves these things. She doesn't deserve to live life feeling the crushing weight of abandonment and guilt from others' emotions. She deserves to live a life of love. To love and be loved without fear. Because there are some things I learned from my evangelical Christian home that I believe in with all my heart: Perfect love casts out fear. And that includes fear of failure because love never fails.

Seeing Red

We have a conspicuous family. At this point, we're pretty used to it. It first started when we adopted our middle child from China at three years old. He was our fourth child (we snuck him in the middle) and at the time also had a six-, five-, and two-year-old. Before the adoption, my wife would go to the park with the kids and no one would bat an eye. What's more American than a white suburban mom out with her three kids?

When we brought home our son, everything changed. Not only did we now have four kids under six years old, but our newest son was from Asia, had cerebral palsy, and couldn't walk on his own. We carried him and he crawled everywhere, at three, four, and even five years old. When he did start to learn how to walk, we had to let him do it on his own. Nothing makes you feel like a terrible parent as much as watching your kid fall down in the middle of Bass Pro Shops, people rushing to his aid and having to say, "He's fine, let him get up by himself."

I remember the first vacation we took after we adopted him. It was eighteen months after we brought him home, and we decided to go to the beach in Galveston, Texas, which is something you do when you're landlocked in Iowa. In hindsight, Texas and the beach seem like a poor choice for a conspicuous family with a child who can't walk. The thing I remember most, though, was swimming in the hotel pool. Our family swam in it for about two to three hours, and the entire time (not an exaggeration) a couple of older folks stared, I mean stared, at my family and my son. It was a tad ridiculous.

But we got used to our conspicuousness quickly, so we *decided* to have another kid (okay, it was a complete accident and before you ask, yes, we know how babies are made). So we had five children, and at this point, all under eight years old.

Towing around five kids, no matter where you go, becomes a circus of sorts. You can't leave kids this young in the car while you run into the gas station for headache medicine. When you do take them somewhere, inevitably one kid will be crying, one will wander off, one will have to be carried, and one will be sleeping. There's usually only one who is listening well at any given time.

But no matter how crazy our life seemed, we got used to it, because that's what you do. People always say things to us like, "I don't know how you do it." Or "I only have two and that's as much as I can handle. I can't imagine five." I like to think this is what the Apostle Paul meant in the Bible when he wrote in his letter to the Corinthians that God will not give you more than you can handle.[46] I'm convinced he was talking about kids. You can't handle it, until you're in it, then you do.

We got used to the craziness, the stares, the looks of pity. So, I decided it was time to come out as transgender to avoid losing our conspicuousness street cred.

This upgraded us to the conspicuous family lifetime membership. We became a family with lesbian parents, one who is transgender, with five kids under ten years old, one who walks with crutches and is Asian, with three out of five being neurodivergent (oh, I forgot to mention that). People in the Midwest stared, mouths agape at us. They'd avert their eyes when we made eye contact. They'd tell us how well-behaved our children were when we went to restaurants, probably because they just assumed we'd be a hot mess based on what they saw when we walked in.

What all this conspicuousness taught us is that where we live matters. Living in a more conservative, less diverse state made us more

---

46 1 Corinthians 10:13.

conspicuous. Something that was highlighted in a documentary we were a part of featuring queer[47] families in the Midwest called, *We Live Here: The Midwest*.[48]

We became acutely aware of this fact a few political seasons ago. In 2019 the Iowa legislature began trying to limit the rights of transgender individuals. There was and still is a concerted effort across conservative states, and now at the federal level, to pass a number of bills limiting the rights of trans children and adults. On the state level, whenever a bill is passed, the language is copied into other conservative state legislatures to try to get it passed there as well.

Where we lived in Iowa, there was a progressive state law, passed in 2007, that afforded protections based on gender identity. Because of that law, I couldn't be discriminated against in hiring, housing, or credit because I am transgender, just like folks can't be discriminated against based on religion or race. Like I said, progressive for 2007. In 2019 however, a group of conservative legislators sponsored a bill to remove gender identity as a protected class in the state code. This to me felt like a huge slap in the face, so I emailed all the Republican sponsors of the bill to ask for a sit down so I could introduce myself and help them understand how this bill could negatively affect my life and my family. To my surprise, three of the legislators took me up on my offer. So, my wife and I went to the state capital and met with them. This was one of the most eye-opening discussions I've had since coming out as a trans woman.

I went into the meeting with few expectations for genuine conversation. I realized immediately getting to the policies would be an uphill battle. Not in terms of these representatives' posture, they were open and there to listen (at least two of them were), but in terms of their knowledge and ignorance on the issue about which they were making a law.

---

47 While I identify as Queer, I want to hold space and recognize that the word has been utilized to marginalize large groups of people in the past.

48 *We Live Here: The Midwest*, directed by Melinda Maerker (Hulu, 2023), https://www.hulu.com/movie/we-live-here-the-midwest.

We shocked them right out of the gate by letting them know that we were indeed married. A transgender married woman, weird, right? Again, we shocked them by making connections in the evangelical Christian community that we were a part of at the time and so were they. A transgender Christian? Impossible. When the topic turned to restrooms, which seemed to be at the crux of the issue for them, they couldn't comprehend what I was telling them. They were hoping to limit the use of restrooms by trans people to the restroom that aligned with sex assigned at birth. So me, assigned male at birth, would have to use the male restroom. They looked at me and I think understood why I wouldn't want to use the men's restroom. When I then told them there would also be trans men, with full beards, hopped up on testosterone, in the women's restroom because of their proposed law, they didn't even get it. What's a trans man?

My story was coming up against the story they were telling themselves about trans people, which fit into their own view of the world. In political terms, we typically see this "story bumping" in terms of winning and losing. If you pass a law that restricts trans people, you and your story about scary trans people wins. And my story about being a woman who most appropriately should use the women's restroom, not the men's, is the loser.

But we need to reframe the conversation. It's not about your story being more valuable than mine or mine being more valuable than yours; it's about us taking care of one another. And me using the women's restroom without fear is you taking care of me.

When it comes to the conservative fight against trans people, the conversation is framed in terms of safety. Women's safety and girls' safety primarily. Me, the scary trans woman (again, we either don't know trans men exist or don't care), assigned male at birth, perhaps with or without a penis, is a threat to safety. When in fact, I am far more likely to be harassed in the restroom than me harassing someone else. And what we're really talking about isn't safety. It is about not wanting to be uncomfortable and keeping a particular view of the world intact. Some people aren't comfortable with me in the restroom. And instead of examining that discomfort, there is a push to legislate their own comfort at the cost of my safety. If I was to be in the women's restroom, seen as a woman, someone's worldview might fall apart, just because a transgender woman is being allowed to be a woman. So, if a law is made that I can't go in there, no one has to think about me or adjust their worldview.

In the end, much of the conversation comes down to restrooms and locker rooms, and it seems to focus on genitals—although so far, laws have stopped short at hiring thousands of genital inspectors for dressing rooms, locker rooms, and restrooms. Ultimately though, if we would truly try to include each other in our respective stories, as I was hoping to do with these state legislators, we wouldn't care about what genitals we have. Instead, we'd listen to understand and empathize, and in the end, we just might learn something.

In 2022, we picked up and moved across the country to Maryland, leaving our home, the only place we'd ever known. Strain from family and friend relationships was hard, but living in a state that didn't have our backs was harder. We decided to go somewhere that explicitly welcomed trans people. Moving across the country with five kids rivaled transitioning genders in terms of a transition for our family, but we aren't conspicuous anymore.

The first day we were in our new home, I went to Home Depot to get paint. When I came home, I had to tell Katie, "Honey, there were TWO other trans women there!" I now realize that I was living with a hum in the background of my life. People looking at me at the gas station, the grocery store, or out to dinner at a restaurant. I was always wondering if someone was going to spot me in the restroom and call the police. I didn't realize that hum was even there until it was gone. Being around so many different races, ethnicities, religions, sexual orientations, and gender identities means differences are normalized.

More people seem to understand we aren't a threat to each other's stories. I can let you be you, and I can be me, and even if we are different, we can both live happily in the same society. Honestly, it's weird. I didn't even realize something like this could exist when I lived in Iowa.

Yes, people have differences of opinion in Maryland. And yes, sometimes people try to make laws to be comfortable rather than to take care of one another, but those laws don't pass. We ask ourselves, what is good for us, and what is good for those who need our help? What can we do to make it better? This type of approach to life and each other was new to me. It makes me a less judgmental person too. I can better hold space for all types of people now, as this new place is holding space for me. It's where my story and your story converge into our story. And it feels like freedom.

The Restroom

With all the above about family conspicuousness, I haven't even mentioned our weirdest kid, our fourth child. We're 86 percent certain he was a higher life form in a past life. Our theory is that, having reached the peak of his civilization, he decided to explore the cosmos and inhabited our unborn child in order to experience humanity. Some of the clues to this origin story are embedded in the way he talks to us and talks about things he experiences in the world.

The first clue he gave us was when he was four years old. I was in my room getting dressed, and he said, "Aren't you going to use the armpit potion?" It caught me by surprise, and I had to think for a second until it occurred to me that he was talking about deodorant! So now each day, I put on my armpit potion, smiling about my little alien and his fascination with our world.

His list of alien exclamations is long.

One night he came running down the stairs while Katie and I were watching television, complaining to us that his "thumb toes" hurt because his footie pajamas were too small.

Once before school as he was getting dressed, he asked if we had washed his "short sleeve pants."

One afternoon I came into the bathroom to find him at the sink, full of water to the brim. When I asked him what was going on, he said that he wanted to see what would happen when the water got to the "sink nostrils."

Our little interstellar traveler is also (like most human children) obsessed with bathroom humor. Farts. Poop. Pee. Bodies going to the bathroom in general. It's all so fascinating to him. And while I'd like to attribute this to the fact that he may be from a galaxy far away, my other four earthbound children are also obsessed. One night as I sat at the dinner table, telling my children maybe a little too vehemently and for the *last time*, no potty talk at the table, I also realized that adults, too, are obsessed. We just take it to the other extreme. We *do not, under any cir-cumstance*, discuss poop, pee, and bodily functions in the bathroom.

In fact, most of us adhere to the social norm of get in, get out, what happens in there stays in there. Being transgender is a unique experience in that I have experienced both men's and women's restroom dynamics, and men's restrooms are much more awkward. First, urinals are essen-tially a torture device for a trans woman. Before I came out, every time I used the urinal, I was reminded that my body did not align with my brain. It also is very uncomfortable when you are a woman to be standing next to men with their genitals in their hands. I'll take a stall any day, thank you. Second, why do men need to make small talk in the restroom? Not the kind of small talk you'd expect, but small talk that is made nowhere else but in the men's restroom. You'll find two men, neither of whom like sports, talking about "the game last night" if they run into each other in the men's restroom.[49] These are just two of the many rea-sons I am grateful for the women's restroom. Although I must say, the chaos of bodily fluids, smells, and sounds in the women's restrooms did come as a surprise to me, someone who thought there might be calming music and couches in each one.

For most trans people though, myself included, using the restroom that corresponds with their gender identity is a significant step, and it can be a significant stressor, especially at the beginning of a gender transition.

---

49 *Saturday Night Live* has a great sketch called "Men's Room." Take a moment and search for it and watch it online; you won't regret it.

I remember the last time I used the men's restroom and decided to start using the women's restroom. I looked much more feminine than masculine and felt safer going into the women's restroom than the men's, so I switched. But even though I felt safer in the women's room, I was terrified every time I had to pee. I remember vividly the human resources conference in Vegas, right after I had come out at work. The conference was at the Las Vegas Convention Center, a massive complex of buildings hosting the annual HR gathering. If you don't know, HR is 70 percent staffed by women. So, as you can imagine, there are lines for the women's restroom at any HR conference. They can get so long that they usually close multiple men's restrooms and convert them to women's restrooms, which they did at this conference. It didn't matter though because the lines were still out the door of each restroom. As a newly out trans woman, the restroom was terrifying, but waiting in line for the restroom was my personal hell. The first day at the conference, I beelined to the help desk to ask where the gender-neutral restroom was in the complex. The lady looked at her map, then got on her walkie to ask the question. "I'm sorry, there isn't one available."

I was stunned. In a complex that big, how was there not one single gender-neutral restroom? So, I sucked it up and walked ten minutes to find a restroom without a line, almost peeing my pants in the process. Days later, on my fourth ask at the help desk, as I hadn't yet been convinced, I was indeed told there was one gender-neutral restroom I could use. But it was almost a full *mile walk* inside the convention complex. I promptly made the walk. But after the thirty minutes it took there and back just to pee, I finally realized I needed to just get in line at the more convenient bathrooms with everyone else. So I did, and as scared as I was, I never looked back.

The narrative that continues to exist around trans women in the restroom makes it very difficult for us to be anything but scared that someone will throw us out as soon as we walk through the door. And that's the best-case scenario in our minds.

Not only do trans women envision other people kicking us out of the restroom, but we also envision a whole host of other nightmare scenarios, including police showing up to inspect our genitals in front of the masses. Or worse, an enraged conservative husband waiting for us outside the restroom to protect "his woman" from the horrors of having to pee next to a trans woman.

In truth, most people don't know or care that I'm a trans woman when I enter the restroom. That's the nice thing about women's restrooms. Most women are wonderfully kind. And if the restroom I am using is in a safe area, once I get over my own fear, it's a place where I can let down, literally and figuratively. And the small talk from women in the restroom is much more pleasant and on par with regular social small talk than it is in the men's restroom. The real-life experience of a trans woman in women's restrooms just doesn't line up with the fear-based discussion around anti-trans laws, much less the hypocrisy of not discussing trans men in men's restrooms.

The Netflix documentary *Disclosure* hits on a big reason why trans women are the focus: the way we have been portrayed in TV and film over the last forty years.[50] The portrayal has always been as gross and perverted, mentally unhinged, the villain, or some combination (think *Ace Ventura*, *Silence of the Lambs*, or *Jerry Springer*).

Laws targeted at this caricature are overreaching and unnecessary, targeting something that doesn't exist. Instead of targeting predators in the women's restrooms (which we already have laws for), they serve to further marginalize trans people and ultimately make it so much more traumatic for us to use the toilet. I just want to poop with the mental space to play Candy Crush, rather than the driving fear that I'll be further ostracized from society because of my need to go in public at a Target store.

We have religious institutions all throughout this country that tell people what they should believe as right and wrong. Many are telling

---

50 *Disclosure*, directed by Sam Feder (Netflix, 2020), https://www.netflix.com/title/81284247.

their members that having an LGBTQ+ identity is something that is sinful and wrong. What then happens to folks in those systems who have LGBTQ+ identities? We hide. And for those who are hiding parts of themselves but have power to make laws, it seems as though they are legislating based on their own shame. There have been a few recent cases where a conservative legislator or governor has been found to be into trans pornography or gay sex, while at the same time trying to make laws restricting trans and gay people. It seems they think that if they legislate LGBTQ+ people out of existence, then they won't have to deal with their own identity and shame. The only way out of this mess is for religious systems to stop shaming people about our identities. Let people be. When we can face our own shame without judgment, then we can finally stop projecting it onto other people.

I have gotten more comfortable in the women's restroom over time, understanding slowly that my own shame and judgment of myself was much more harsh than other people's judgment of me. I remember the first time I stopped and looked at myself in the mirror to fix my hair in the women's restroom. It was *two years* after I had started using the women's restroom. I finally felt comfortable enough to linger for an extra few seconds to make sure I looked okay before giving a presentation. The more time passes, the more I understand, people are people, and we all just want to use the restroom in peace. We all want to pretend that none of us fart, and we all just want to live our lives, which sometimes includes unpredictable bowel movements.

We should all take a lesson from my (potentially) alien son: normalize talking about the restroom. Don't be scared. We don't have to be crude, but the more we shed light on how we're feeling while we're in there, especially as trans people, the better chance we have at discovering our shared humanity and dispelling our shame together.

A Hope Gone

It's been almost four years since I came out. A lot has changed in those years. Many predictable changes.

My hair is longer, my kids are older, and I am more comfortable shopping in the women's section at Target (or anywhere for that matter). I rarely get misgendered when I'm out and about and have met many people who didn't know me before I transitioned and therefore can't deadname me even if they wanted to.

There have been some surprising changes too. My feet are smaller (weird musculoskeletal side effect, right?). My faith doesn't define my whole life like it used to and looks much different. And every day I am surprised by the generosity and love of strangers and friends in ways I have never experienced before. Somehow showing more of my vulnerability and humanity to others has made it possible for others to show more of their vulnerability and humanity to me.

It surprises me less and less though, because the biggest thing I've learned in the last few years is to let go of my own judgment. Of myself and of other people.

When I came out, even those times I did it somewhat impulsively, I predicted with each letter tentatively sent to friends and loved ones who would be supportive of me and who would end our relationship. It's a game my psyche liked to play to try to protect itself, mostly on the negative side. If I thought a person would reject me, it would make it easier when it did happen.

What I learned though, to quote Ted Lasso, is that, "All people are different people."[51] There really is no predicting who will let us down and who won't. And trying to guess is really our (my) own judgment of that person. Now when I talk to someone about who I am, I am better at holding space. I let them tell me what they think, I let them tell me about who they are, with both their words and actions, before making a judgment call as to whether I should be in a relationship with them. I make room for their story hoping they make room for mine.

Today I feel that judgment again. I sent an email to my parents letting them know I wanted to see them and needed them to respect me and my name, for my sake and the sake of my kids who know me as their Mommo—one of the two moms they have, not their dad.

I got back a response which essentially shut the door on relationship. We can't do it, they said. Period.

Hope of reconciliation with my parents, for the first time, is gone. It's a weird feeling. Hope was keeping me going. But at the same time, now that it's gone, I feel like it was holding me back too.

Every move I made, everything I did, I still was thinking about how my parents would perceive it and whether it would make them more or less likely to be back in a relationship with me. That's no way to live life.

And while that hope initially allowed me to come out, now, without that hope, I can be me, without judgment from people who I am not even in a relationship with. Do I want to be in a relationship with them? Of course. Do I have hopes that it will happen in the future? No, I don't anymore, and I'm okay with that.

I know they love me in the only way they know how, and even though it doesn't feel loving to me, I'll continue to include them in my

---

51 *Ted Lasso*, season 2, episode 1, "Goodbye Earl," directed by Declan Lowney, aired July 23, 2021, AppleTV, https://tv.apple.com/us/episode/goodbye-earl/.

story. Because they were an integral part of my life growing up, making me who I am today. And I love them and thank them for that.

And while I don't hold out hope anymore that I'll be able to tell them that, I do hope that they know.

Faith of a Child

When I started writing, I was in a crisis of faith. Or at least I thought I was in a crisis of faith. As it turns out, all I had to do was look inward because God was inside all along. I've known this since I was a kid. Since I was out in the woods with Casey, experiencing the world in its raw state. As a kid, I realized the things the church was telling me weren't always compatible with what I knew to be true about God and the world. So, I started asking the questions, how would I describe God and how is God reflected in me?

How you might answer these questions depends greatly on who you are, where you come from, what experiences you've had, and what you're currently experiencing. Our view of God is nothing less than our experience of the world around us. It is our experience of God through reading ancient texts, knowing other people, finding solitude, and living everyday life.

Unfortunately, religion tells us to label our experiences as good or bad. Or in the case of a redemptive story, bad leading to good. In my church, we tended to categorize our experiences into good and bad and then label them as truly God, or truly not. No matter how we label them though, our experiences inform our view of who God is.

You may be familiar with the story of the blind men and the elephant.[52] If not, I'll get you caught up.

---

52 Also called "The Elephant in the Dark." For more, check out the Wikipedia page, https://en.wikipedia.org/wiki/Blind_men_and_an_elephant.

Once upon a time, there lived six blind men in a village. One day the villagers told them, "Hey, there is an elephant in the village today." The men had no idea what an elephant was, so they decided, "Even though we would not be able to see it, let us go and feel it anyway." All of them went where the elephant was, and every one of them touched the elephant.

"Hey, the elephant is a pillar," said the first man who touched the elephant's leg.

"Oh, no! It is like a rope," said the second man who touched the elephant's tail.

"Oh, no! It is like a thick branch of a tree," said the third man who touched the elephant's trunk.

"It is like a big hand fan," said the fourth man who touched the elephant's ear.

"It is like a huge wall," said the fifth man who touched the elephant's belly.

"It is like a solid pipe," said the sixth man who touched the elephant's tusk.

They began to argue about the elephant, and every one of them insisted he was right. A man was passing by and he heard the men's agitation. He stopped and asked them, "What is the matter?" They said, "We cannot agree to what the elephant is like." Each one of them told what he thought the elephant was like. The man calmly explained to them, "All of you are right. The reason every one of you is telling it differently is because each one of you touched a different part of the elephant. The elephant is all of what you said."

This story originated on the ancient Indian subcontinent. And before you categorize this story as good or bad, let me tell you it's already been done. It's been adapted to many cultures as a good example of how to see other perspectives. However, I also found an article online called

"3 Ways The Blind Men and the Elephant Story Backfires," labeling the story as heretical to the Christian faith.[53]

I was reading recently in *Lies We Believe About God*, by Wm. Paul Young, that the Greek word for *accuse*, which the Bible uses for Satan, the accuser, is *kategoro*.[54] This is where we get the word *categorize*. Our brains want to label and categorize, which is important for survival. Is that a stick? Or is that a deadly cobra? What category is it in? But when our categorizations start to place unreasonable judgment, value, and worth on the thing categorized, we join the accuser, the adversary of our humanity.

When it comes to categorizing people, Jesus showed us there is no in, and there is no out: there is only us.

The Christian tradition has Jesus, someone who helps us with that fuller picture of who God is. We have many others throughout history that illuminate God to us in ways we never thought possible. When we open ourselves up to the experiences of others, our concept of who we think God is may dissolve entirely like mine has. And in order to stabilize myself from the freefall of a deconstructing faith, I just had to look inward.

When I was a devout evangelical, check-the-boxes Christian, one thing I could never connect with was God's humanity. We said the phrase "God's will for your life" a lot. It was a phrase we threw around loosely, and in most Christian circles, it implies God has a specific will, which means I should make correct decisions to stay in that will. There is a power dynamic. God is there watching, and I am here making decisions, hoping they are right. Me human, God divine.

---

53 Trevin Wax, "3 Ways 'The Blind Men and the Elephant' Story Backfires," *The Gospel Coalition*, August 25, 2016, https://www.thegospelcoalition.org/blogs/trevin-wax/3-ways-the-blind-men-and-the-elephant-story-backfires/.

54 Wm. Paul Young, *Lies We Believe About God* (Atria Books, 2017).

Then during a church service years back, I heard someone use the phrase "Eyes to see like God sees." I honestly can't even remember the context.

I prayed with all my heart, "God, I want to have eyes to see like you see. I, down here, want to see what you see from up there." I didn't even realize the paradigm of *God up there, I down here* that I was so used to until I got this internal response from my prayer:

"Your eyes are my eyes. How else do you think I see?"

I thought, *No, God, you see everything. You see from above the whole picture at the same time.*

Again, the response from within was, "No, what you see, I see. What you feel, I feel."

I was blown away. Not only do I have access to God's perspective, every day, all the time, but God feels what I feel. God human, me divine. The God-in-me empowerment.

Just like my experience at the Center for Action and Contemplation, I had what I needed inside me all along. It almost feels cliché, like the end of every coming-of-age story where our hero realizes they themselves have the power to control their own destiny, but it's true. What we need is inside us. And when we let it out, it shines. Not pointing the way to the "one true God" like I used to think, but giving a fuller picture of who we are as humans inside of a greater, vast universe. It gives us a fuller picture of who we are and how we work together in symbiosis, for the greater good of humanity and each other. This is the Divine.

For the first time in my life, I feel like I have everything I need. And I just needed to look within the whole time. Or maybe head back out into the woods.

Yet Love Grows

I need to get out in nature. I need to feel something. I have emotions inside me that I just can't get out.

My dad just died.

I haven't seen him in a year, and although our relationship was strained, I did get to meet him and catch up more often than most of my other relatives. We'd meet at a Perkins restaurant, his favorite spot, and we'd exchange the usual perfunctory "How's it going" before the conversation devolved into a conversation about faith, disappointment, and how my dad perceived me being trans as sinful. It was rough, but it was something.

The last conversation I had with him was good until it wasn't. He asked me why I hated the church. I told him the truth, that I didn't. While organized religion has hurt me more than words can say, it informed the person I am now. It's my homeland, and maybe most importantly, it taught me how to love. My dad taught me how to love. I tried to get my point across that you can both be hurt by something and appreciate what it has given you. It doesn't mean that you have to continually enter back into that relationship and be hurt over and over.

My father looked frail at our last meeting, so I made one last attempt, selfishly, to feel loved. As we were headed out, once we got to the parking lot, I looked at him and abruptly asked, "Do you want me at your funeral?"

To the average person, this may seem like a morbid question, but if you were to know my father, you would know he had been planning his funeral for the last thirty years, especially after he had a major heart attack in his early forties. At the time, I didn't know what was happening and was scared, but everyone said it was going to be okay. He lived, but everything changed. My mom became a caretaker, and my dad, seeing his own mortality up close, became obsessed with it. He and my mom bought funeral plots and started to plan everything out. By the time my dad died, he had a lockbox full of instructions for his funeral, down to scripting the preacher's words for the service. He just had so much time to think about his death that he was on draft forty-five of his funeral plans, with no details left to mull over.

I asked that question there in the parking lot, and he paused and looked at me and said, "I don't know. Maybe, if you cannot make it all about you." Oof. I wasn't exactly sure what that meant, but it seemed as though he meant, if you cannot be a woman at my funeral. I said okay, and we parted ways for the last time.

My attempt to find love in the parking lot with my dad didn't really matter in the end because when you're dead, try as you might, you can't control things anymore. My mom prohibited me from going to the funeral. She told me through my in-laws. She said it was his wish. Maybe it was, or maybe she couldn't face it either. I asked to come back the day before to see his body and say goodbye. The only reason I was able to do so is because my brother fought hard for me. I thank him for that.

Coming the morning of the funeral to an empty room, seeing my dad lying there, was hard. Knowing he was truly a good man, and knowing we now never had a chance to fix what was broken. My brother joined me in the room and we cried and hugged.

The funeral slideshow and materials denied my existence. It hurt. It hurt even more that I never even got a picture of my true self with my dad. In the five years since I came out, we never took one picture together.

Looking back, I'm disappointed. Sometimes I wish I would have pushed harder to be seen. But this wouldn't have been fair. It wouldn't have been loving to him. Because love lets others view us how they want to view us. In the end that meant I had to put up my boundary and he had to put up his, but my love still grew for him. And at that far distance, our love for each other could exist and hopefully grow.

I headed out of that funeral home to a waiting friend who took me to Perkins to celebrate my father's life in my own way. In the airline concourse later that morning, I pulled up the live stream of my dad's funeral. My brother gave a wonderfully funny eulogy (I am typically the funny speech giver in the family, so kudos to him for stepping up big). The preacher talked about my dad wanting to control his funeral and everyone there laughed because they all knew how he made his ending a big part of his living. And that was it.

After I got home, I talked to my dad, knowing that he was in a place without the pain and heart ailments he had been enduring, and my love for him grew.

It's now been over six years since I came out to my family. Six years since my life changed forever. I don't hold out hope that my mom and sister will come to see me differently, but I still reach out. I so strongly believe in the power of love that I think there is a way through the rhetoric and religion to get to the heart of the matter. We were family. We are family.

I contacted my mom recently as we were headed back to Iowa for a visit, and I asked if I could bring the dog over and say hi. I wanted to just have a nice, surface-level chat, something we've been unable to do for so long. I let my boundary down and reached out. I was met with the same conversations we've had before. Pain. It didn't used to be like this. As adults, my siblings and spouses and Katie and I used to visit my parents' house every Sunday, where my mom loved playing with her grandkids and making food for us all, her way of sharing her love.

But now the texts have stopped. She drew a boundary. I had drawn boundaries. We are farther apart than ever. Yet this is the distance at which love can still grow. At this point in time, if we were to be closer to one another, we would both be hurt more.

I can respect my mom from this distance. Not agree with her but respect her and her boundary, as I likewise created my own boundary. When we respect the boundary someone else gives us, there is room for love. I love my mom and I want to continue to feel that. Maybe someday, she can love me too. Me as I am now. I know, it's starting to sound like hope again, isn't it?

For now, I'll sit at a distance, hurting, waiting, loving, full of joy, sometimes pain, just living my life, doing my best to let my love grow.

Contentment

I woke up today: content. Now that I think about it, I've been content for a while. Maybe it's the fact that it's Thanksgiving today and since I was a kid, I've been told to count my blessings. More likely, it's the fact that I have a four-day weekend and have some time to breathe between everything that's going on in my life and the world (five kids, master's program, writing a TV pilot, and my work in human resources).

Either way, I like this feeling of contentment. It's something I haven't found in a sustained way in a long time. In the past six years since I started writing about my experiences, there have been a whirlwind of emotions. Ups and downs, but many strong, intense, and what we as humans perceive as negative emotions. Sadness, anger, fear, despair, dysphoria. But today I realize that I am content precisely because I have been able to feel all those things. The emotional work I've done has led me to this place of contentment.

It's a nice place actually. I really feel like maybe I should unpack my bags and stay awhile. For the first time in my life, I'm content with my body. I'm not distraught when I see my naked reflection in the mirror. Yes, I had gender confirmation surgery which goes a long way, and yes, I still find flaws with my body just like everyone else, but this feels like the contentment is mine. I own it. A few months before I had gender confirmation surgery, I found a local photographer who I trusted to do a nude photo shoot. I wanted to honor my body, pay homage to what it had given me so far, feel at home with it, even while I knew I might not ever feel fully at home, even after surgery. But now, I do feel at home. And I credit a lot of my contentment to that photo shoot. It helped me let go of judgment. Baring myself, even the parts of me I wasn't comfortable with, for my photographer to see, and to have those images in perpetuity helped me see the beauty that was always there. I let go of the judgment of what I think my trans body should or should not be and instead just let her be.

Moving far from my hometown, my place of origin, has helped too. For the first time in my life, I can walk through the grocery store without constantly wondering about what others are thinking about me. Yes, I still have those days, but they are few and far between. Quite frankly it's bizarre to be looking for pumpkin spice to put in my . . . everything, and be thinking only about which aisle shelves the pumpkin spice. For the first thirty-five years of my life, I would walk into a grocery store afraid that someone would find out my secret. Afraid to talk to anyone, afraid to make eye contact with anyone, moving quickly through the store with my head down, moving so fast that I could have been mistaken for a champion power walker. Now that I think about it, I did take power walking and jogging as a class in college, so maybe I was unconsciously trying to increase my superhuman abilities to not be noticed in the grocery store.

When I came out publicly, my thoughts changed, from hiding to judging. Judging who was judging me. Why were they staring? Was it because I don't blend in with the other women? Am I too tall? Are my shoulders too broad? Is my makeup done terribly? Are my clothes giving me away? I was terrified to speak anywhere I went, understanding that it would automatically bring judgment down on me. For me, in my Iowa-nice rural town near the liberal capital city, it was less about safety and more about judgment. I didn't want to speak because I didn't want to be judged. I went from blending in and not being seen, to sticking out like a sore thumb. Thinking about others the whole time.

But now I've moved away. I had that photo shoot and another shoot after my surgery, and things have changed. I'm learning to drop my own judgment of myself, daily, and in turn, I'm learning to drop others' judgment of me.

I was recently talking to a friend about decorating their house, and they were telling me how they would decorate it now that they were getting a divorce and would be in control of all the decorating decisions. At one point, they were overwhelmed by the process, and I said, "Don't worry, you just need to do what makes you feel happy." They responded with, "But what if other people don't like it?" I said, "It doesn't matter if others don't like it, it only matters if you like it!" Their response was telling, something many of us think but aren't saying out loud. They said, "Is that really true? Because I think about the judgment of others in all the decisions I make." They weren't saying they didn't like this about themself, but more stating this is the way it is.

For many of us, trans or not, that is the way it is. We move through the world based on how we're judged by others. Bouncing from one decision to the next, collecting the judgment from moms, dads, siblings, relatives, friends, and strangers, putting these ways of being in a fanny pack around our waist, until it tips us over onto our faces and we're lying face down on the ground from the weight of all the judgment.

Dropping other people's judgment or perceived judgment of me has only come since I've started to drop the judgment of myself, and since I've started to understand boundaries.

Contentment and boundaries are inextricably linked. Boundaries have been hard for me because I am a peacemaker, someone who at heart wants other people to feel seen and loved. So when I used to clash with someone, my default would be to defer to them and move forward in relationship. This was not a healthy way to move through the world, but it was my base ego, my default, my adaptive self. It's how my personality has protected me throughout my life and, for a time, has served me. But as I started to break down my own ego, I realized I needed to understand boundaries more fully.

When I first came out, I didn't understand boundaries and was not ready to implement them in my life. The act of coming out itself, though, became a first big step in understanding what it was like to say to someone, "No, you can't treat me this way anymore." Even though no one should be blamed for seeing me or treating me like a man, it was a boundary moment for me to say, "No, I am a woman, please respond accordingly." For those who said yes to my boundary, for those who respected who I am and showed me through their actions and words, they showed me what love was. They showed me I was worthy of being honored. And with each person who honored me with love and respect, they revealed a little bit more of me to myself. They taught me that, yes, I am worthy of honor, love, and respect. Yes, others should treat me this way. Yes, I should treat myself this way. They set the bar.

When I came out at our church, there were many people who wanted to discuss the theological ideas around whether our church should be affirming trans people or not. For me, I had wrestled with those ideas all my life and finally had to put them aside, understanding that I was a human being worthy of love, period. When others wanted to continue to talk through why they thought the Bible said I shouldn't be trans, I had to say no. It wasn't respectful to me and wasn't healthy for me in the long run. Boundaries double down in that way. The more you implement them, the more you love and respect yourself, the more you can drop your own judgment and ignore the others judging you, the more you love and respect yourself, the more you can implement healthy boundaries. I add the word *healthy* because there seems to be a fine line between healthy boundaries and unhealthy relational expectations where we expect others to cater to our needs or discomfort.

For those who refuse to respect my boundaries, such as calling me by my actual name, they've in turn accused me of not respecting their boundaries. I say I can only be in a relationship if they respect and honor me by using my name and pronouns; they say they can only be in a relationship if they're able to call me by whatever name and pronouns they choose.

This gets tricky because while these two things sound the same, there are major differences. My boundary says, "This is who I am in relationship to you, and I get to define me in that relationship. I will determine how I exist and behave in the world, and this is what I need from you." The boundary from the one refusing to use my name says, "This is who you are in relationship to me; I get to define you and how you exist and behave in the world, and this is what I need you to be for me." The unhealthy boundary essentially says, "My belief about you is more important than your belief about yourself, and I get to define your story so it fits in with mine." Whereas the healthy boundary says, "My belief about me and your belief about you are both important, and we each get to define our own stories."

To maintain a healthy boundary, first, we must do the work to know ourselves, what our identities are, how we describe ourselves, how we see the world, and what our preferences are. The more we do this kind of digging and hard ego work, we may be surprised how our belief about ourselves wasn't built on anything real to begin with and has the ability to change. In doing the work, we will come to understand that the more work we do, the more we will uncover who we are at the core of ourselves.

Second, we need to be willing to tell someone about who we are. By sharing our story and our place in the world, we expose ourselves to rejection and hurt but become surer of who we are after doing the work. We open ourselves to this possibility in the vulnerability of sharing.

Next is where healthy and unhealthy boundaries diverge. Having done the work to know ourselves, we can find solutions that we are comfortable with that still feel honoring to our story. We can find solutions for how we can exist and behave in the world in relationship with others. If others haven't done their work, they often offer a different solution. They offer a solution that privileges them in defining how we exist and behave in the world, thinking we should conform to their story to exist in the world. It's still a boundary, but an unhealthy one that doesn't focus on defining themselves and instead focuses on defining us.

I am only able to create boundaries in my life now because I have done a shit ton of personal work. I dig with my therapist, I dig with my spouse, I dig with my friends, I dig until I hit the core of me. Each time uncovering more pieces of myself, getting a fuller picture. This is why I now know that I deserve respect and dignity. You need to call me by my name and use my correct pronouns. This is the baseline for any relationship.

My work has led me to have confidence in who I am. It allowed me to come out, and as an out trans woman, it allows me to open myself every day to rejection from others in my vulnerability. When I say this is how I define me, it gives others the opportunity to say, well, we don't see you that way.

In my self-differentiation, it is okay if someone doesn't see me how I see me. It's their prerogative. And if they hold a boundary, however unhealthy, and try to define me in a way that I know isn't compatible with who I am, then I respect their boundary by telling them we can't be in a relationship. This is why most people I'm not in a relationship with today think that I cut off relationship with them. What they don't understand is, I want a relationship. I just want the basic right to define myself. Them defining me is a nonstarter. I still want others to be seen and heard for who they are, I just no longer will allow people to not see me for who I am.

Letting go of the need to defer to the other person in my relationships and learning to hold healthy boundaries has been life-giving. All the pain and heartache that comes from doing life without someone you care about has led me to contentment with who I am in relation to others and in relationship to the universe.

And the more people I meet, the more I uncover things about myself. I keep learning about the unique stories of other people in this world, and it expands my own story, it busts my box open even wider. At this point, I understand that who I am as a trans woman, or for many other reasons, may not be compatible with who you want me to be, and that's okay.

Am I done with gender transition? Maybe. I don't know for sure. But what I do know is that transition will always be a part of my life because I want the moments that lead to transformation, whatever they may be. I want growth to be a part of my life. I want love to lead the way. And when I do that, truly all manner of things can happen. I can build a beautiful relationship with a partner. I can be friends with someone where we know each other deep down. I can sit across from someone with a different ideology and open myself up to them, finding mutual respect for one another. I can bump into a stranger on the street and our stories can connect. And leading with love, I can empathize and understand when people don't want to be around me because of their own beliefs about themselves.

This is me. For much of my life, I hardly knew me, but now I know myself and am confident in my own Knowing. I'm confident in the fact that I know I don't know everything and never will. I'm confident in my idea that if I keep growing, I'll keep knowing and unknowing at the same time, leading me to a more lovely and beautiful life. And these are some of the moments that got me to where I am today. I'm glad my story got to bump into yours in this world. I hope we get to experience more of each other in the future.

Life as It Is (Epilogue)

I'm up again in the early morning. This time with an aging dog, not with emotions banging around to get out. Life is content. It's being known. It's something that is easily pictured, though what comes next is always a surprise. I take the kids to soccer, theater, and band. I go get coffee with Katie every Saturday morning, and I still get smoothies on Friday. It's a place I love to be. It's a place where privilege matters less (though I still have a lot) and internal stability is much more important. Even sitting inside broken relationships, the peace I feel is palpable. It's a place where hate and judgment have virtually disappeared out of my daily life, my own judgment of myself included.

People don't stare anymore. My kids have to answer curious questions from their friends about their two moms, one of whom is trans, but they love answering them and are good at it. They truly know what love is because they have two present parents instead of one. They know what freedom looks like and why boundaries are important, understanding that relationships are nuanced.

I expose my true self to everyone. I have nothing to hide. I become more effective in helping people find and live into their true selves. Although I'm working with mostly queer people, I enjoy meeting all types of new people everywhere I go. People know I'm transgender, but it's not my whole identity. I am still a soul, part of the cosmos, one of many, where ultimately gender doesn't matter. I'm in my early forties, embraced by most humans in real life and only ridiculed by trolls online.

Yes, life is hard sometimes and broken relationships still weigh on me from time to time, but I enjoy living. I tried to volunteer to coach my son's soccer team a few weeks ago, and everyone wanted me to do it because they needed a coach, but I was in the middle of writing a book, so I will next year. My kids have two moms, and that is something that is a part of their life but doesn't define who they are, each of them individual and unique. I can still teach them to fish, shave, ride a bike, play video games, and I can be who I am with them. I'm excited to age and get to fifty and watch them graduate. I know they would be different people had I not come out when I did. They'd be smaller, less exposed to the world, less willing to try new things and meet new people.

I am doing more writing and speaking, even in my forties. I travel with Katie and the kids, mostly for pleasure, and love meeting new people wherever we go. My world is open. I am open. My soul is free. I know that when I die, no matter if I make it to be an old woman, I will have lived a full life. I already have. I understand love and suffering. I know I haven't limited myself by the choices I made (adoption, church leadership, relationships, coming out), but they have helped me grow and remain open to the world. They have made me who I am today.

I know I am loved by many, a divine love that courses through my body. I know Love so intimately, all because of the amazing relationships and the self-love and Knowing that I have gained along the way. I don't know what the future holds, but I know that if I stay true to who I am and continue to surround myself by people who love me, life as it will be in the future is full of unlimited possibilities.

Acknowledgments

Over the past eight years, the road that led to this book was built by letting out emotions during key moments of my life. During those moments, both celebratory and painful, there was almost always someone there to celebrate with me or to sit with me in my grief and pain. Thank you to everyone who I saw along that road, with a special thanks to a few people who were there along the way.

Kristin, it feels like we've known each other our whole lives and maybe a few lives before this one. I'm so glad that being my true self allowed us to find each other. Your love and support is indescribable. You mean the world to me, and I wouldn't be here without you.

Tree, I look back on our first travels together like they were a million years ago, and it also feels like yesterday. Thanks for the symbiosis that is living life together with you.

Sami, you've been there for me since day one, and your support has allowed me and our family to be ourselves. Love you.

Chris and Sarah, thank you for fighting for me even when it put you in the middle of something hard. Your love has been felt.

ABQ Gang of Seven and Lindsey and Amma, your presence and care during that life-changing conference in Albuquerque has been invaluable and something I will forever cherish.

Casey, your friendship in our formative years will stay with me for the rest of our lives. I can't wait to see you again and go for a hike in the woods.

Resisterhood, you all breathed life into me at the most pivotal turning points. You affirmed who I am from the start and welcomed me in, giving me the confidence to live in a world that sometimes makes me feel like I'm not welcome.

Erin and CJ, you are truly what it means to be found family. I'm so glad we're able to live life together. Thank you for your support and more importantly your familyship.

To the family that I've lost, I hope we can see each other again someday. You've made me the person I am today. And to my dad, may you rest in peace knowing that I think of you every time I see a bag of circus peanuts.

Thank you, David and team at Lake Drive Books, for being a thought partner seeing something in my original, messy, emotional writings. Your insight and care has been felt, and I'm so grateful for your guidance along the way.

To my kids, R, L, C, J, and E, you are the loves of my life. I know a lot has been thrown at you in the past few years, and I am so amazed at your resilience and love that you have continued to show. Your growth amazes me and gives me something to strive for. I love you!

And Katie, from that first concert, I knew you were something special. My being is full from the love I have felt from you and feel for you. You are my favorite. A & K All the Way!!!

About the Author

Nia Chiaramonte, with her wife Katie J. Chiaramonte, is the co-founder of Love in the Face (loveintheface.com) and co-author of *Embracing Queer Family: Learning to Live Authentically in Our Families and Communities*. Nia and Katie work to support other transgender and LGBTQIA+ individuals and their families on their journeys of self-discovery. She and Katie were featured in the Hulu documentary *We Live Here*. Nia is a nonprofit professional, and she and Katie reside near Baltimore, Maryland with their five children.

About Lake Drive Books

Lake Drive Books is an independent publishing company offering books that help you heal, grow, and discover. We champion books about values and strategies, not ideologies, and authors who are spiritually rich, contextually intelligent, and focused on human flourishing. We want to help readers feel seen.

If you like this or any of our other books at lakedrivebooks.com, we could use your help: please follow our authors on social media, subscribe to their newsletters, and tell others what you think of their remarkable books.